From Ghetto to Glory

The Real Life Story of Job

Asim Suah Khalfani

authorHOUSE®

AuthorHouse™
1663 Liberty Drive
Bloomington, IN 47403
www.authorhouse.com
Phone: 1 (800) 839-8640

Published by AuthorHouse 04/25/2016

ISBN: 978-1-5246-8927-8 (sc)
ISBN: 978-1-5246-8925-4 (hc)
ISBN: 978-1-5246-8926-1 (e)

Library of Congress Control Number: 2017906284

Print information available on the last page.

CONTENTS

This Is Dedicated to my TWO FIRST LOVES.

> *"no weapon forged against you will prevail, and you will refute every tongue that accuses you. This is the heritage of the servants of the Lord, and this is their vindication from me," declares the Lord."*
>
> Isaiah 54:17 NIV

Mae . Your quick witty comebacks and philosophy on life has been two of the things that I remembered most about you and have adopted for my own life to this day.

Yvette. Your kindhearted spirit and tenacious attitude to never count you out of any situation I live by daily. I demonstrated it on and off the gridiron and now in the daily interactions with individuals that I come in contact with.

No Charge

This song use to play on my momma's radio as she would drive me to daycare.

There is no charge
When you add it all up the real cost of my love
Is no charge
For the nights filled with dred
And the worries ahead, no charge
For the advice and the knowledge
And the costs of your college, no charge
For the toys, food and clothes
And for wiping your nose there's no charge son
When you add it all up the real cost of my love
Is no charge

Before we start this journey, I have to lay down the foundation. I think these individuals have been the potters who molded and shaped this sculpture that people interact with on a daily basis. I have to give credit where credit is due.

First my grandmother, Miss Mae. Your name, Mae, means savior. A woman who was kind, sincere, stern, witty and funny all at the same time. Even though I only knew you for the first six years of my life, you laid down an awesome foundation that I still use to this day. You taught me to play by myself if those around me aren't doing the things that are what I'm wanting to do. You was the first person who taught me to never be afraid to go against the grain and go off on my own even if it means being an outcast in the group.

1

Second is, your daughter, my mother, Miss Yvette. Your name, Yvette, means helper of mankind, and that's what you were. You were my heart, my world, my everything.

Where do I begin?

You showed me how despite where you begin in life that doesn't mean that's where you have to finish. Though you was a single parent living in one of the worst projects in Winston-Salem and raising 3 kids on your own, you never complained nor griped about the cards that were dealt to you. I watched you for 19 years do it and do it BIG. You where my mother, my father, my magician pulling off magic tricks and illusions while working only one job to feed three kids (one having an appetite that'll put Ci Ci pizza outta business). You went on to put one through college, who became the first to receive a college degree in the family. We never had a bad Christmas. Everything we asked for we got on our Christmas list. You made sure of that. Plain and simple. Momma, I never had a chance to tell you this but you were so good with playing the magician role that I didn't realize how poor we really were until the fall semester of my freshman year because we had a plethora of things in comparison to some of my friends-your love, food on the table (name brand food top shelf), clothes, toys, a ceiling fan and an air condition, a lawn mower, a car, two televisions, a VCR with a plethora of VHS tapes, cable channels with HBO, and Cinemax, we were encouraged to play sports even if it didn't fit into the non-existing budget. Your 'never quit-never surrender' spirit is one that has kept me sane through all the trials and tribulations that I've gone through throughout this journey.

The rose that grew from the concrete.

You taught me how to set my mind on something and not to quit until I got it or accomplished it PERIOD. It wasn't until your death that when cleaning out your top dresser drawer that I found something that said you only completed the 12th grade.

You couldn't have told me you hadn't started or went to college.

But that's just it. A chameleon able to adapt and blend in with her surroundings and hold a conversation with the best of them. A great magician never reveals their secrets to their tricks. They keep the audience engaged at all times.

Momma I promise your baby boy is going to make a splash in this world and contribute to making it a better place. The world hasn't seen what's about to take place. When we (you, grandma, and me) meet again, I know you two will be so proud of your baby boy.

My wife will have some the same characteristics that you two ladies took the time to share and instill in me in the short amount of time I knew you two.

I thank God for assigning me two beautiful wonderful women who started me down a road that has been crazy, scary, and interesting. It has been times I wanted to pack up my stuff and just quit but that's not 'The way'.

AND LAST BUT NOT LEAST

Saving the Best for last. Thank you Abba Father for never giving up on me and loving me when I sometimes couldn't or didn't understand how to love myself. You NEVER left me nor forsake me. Like your word said in Jeremiah *"For I know the plans I have for you,"* declares the Lord, *plans to prosper you and not to harm you, plans to give you hope and a future.* Jer.29.11.niv.

Your word has kept me and has been my rock in tough times, my manna during this Job-like roller coaster ride especially this last trial. I've learn to understand and apply what your word means and to hold on to your word even when the physical is contradicting the spiritual. Psalms 103:3 says *who forgives all your sins and heals all your diseases* and Jeremiah 30:17 *"But I will restore you to health and heal your wounds,' declares the Lord, 'because you are called an outcast, Zion for whom no one cares.'"*

> And how can I forget Isaiah 53:4-5 *"Surely he took up our pain and bore our suffering, yet we considered him punished by God, stricken by him, and afflicted. But he was pierced for our transgressions, he was crushed for our iniquities; the punishment that brought us peace was on him, and by his wounds we are healed."*
>
> Isaiah 53:4-5 NIV

Looking back over the years I now see another passage unveiled as well in Jeremiah where it says

"Before I formed you in the womb I knew you, before you were born I set you apart; I appointed you as a prophet to the nations."

jer.1:5 NIV

It's amazing how when you put Him first, how everything just falls in its respective place perfectly like a jigsaw puzzle with no mistake or chaos.

You knew me way before I ever got here! Thank you my God. My Father. My Healer. My Provider. My Peace & Victory. My EVERY THING.

Well, you know when I think about No charge I think about the day that Jesus went out on Calvary died for me; gave His life as a ransom for me

My debt was paid in full.

When you add it all up the real cost of real love is no charge.

Thank you guys.
I'm forever indebted to all 3 of you.
Bill PAID IN FULL!
Your love for me was NO CHARGE!

THE CLIFF NOTES OF
THE BOOK OF JOB

In the book of Job, Job was tested on three separate occasions from the devil. He tried to prove to God that Job would curse Him and turn away from Him. The devil thought that the only reason Job was faithful was because God had blessed him tremendously and that there was a hedge and protective barrier around him that prevented the devil from getting close to Job. Then God granted him permission on the three separate occasions to allow the devil to test Job but there was only ONE CONDITION -The devil COULD NOT take Job's life.

The three tests Job experienced were as follows:

Test #1. Job lost ALL his kids. They were killed when a vicious wind blew through knocking over the four walls of the house and killing them.

Test #2. All of Job's possessions were taken from him in a single day. While his servants were out in the fields, raiders came and killed all the servants but one and took all the livestock and Job's possessions. The one that lived got away to run to tell Job what had happened.

Test #3. Job health was terribly affected to the point where those who knew him didn't even recognize him. He had boils starting from his head down to his feet.

His close friends advised him that the trials he were experiencing were because God was punishing him for some evil deed or deeds he had committed.

Heck his own wife even encourage him "to curse God and die" with all the bad stuff that was happening to him. Even though Job experience the

3 trials, Job stayed faithful and believed that God would see him through inspite of it all.

> *After Job had prayed for his friends, the Lord restored his fortunes and gave him twice as much as he had before.* Job 42:10 NIV

THE SHOW

Life to me is nothing but a big movie with a soundtrack of various songs that take you back to a particular period in your life aka your movie.

God is the director, producer, and script writer.

My job is to act. When it's time to get on stage and perform, He lets me know. When it's my time to get wrote off the show, He again let's me know.

On some occasions we may try to exit without His consent and He makes us stay on the set until we get it right, and other times we show up for work to find out when we read our script our part has been written off the show without us or the supporting casts knowing. But that's how G operates because honestly it's His show. We have to learn how to ad lib with the script and work with what's been giving to us with the props and supporting cast.

A lot of times when my sisters and I get together we are always laughing and quoting scenes from various movies and standup comedy routines. So I thought it would be fitting to name some of the chapters, titles of movies and songs throughout the book. I guess you can say this is my small dedication also to two of my best movie buff partners in the household.

So buckle up and 'pass me those peas cause Sophia is home! (Line from *The Color Purple)*

Get your popcorn ready and sit back and get ready for an exciting trip of the real life story of Asim Suah Khalfani, and how my life is similar or parallel to one of the most tested people in the bible, Job. Before I start, there are some experiences that I have experienced that Job didn't go through or are not recorded in the bible that are my own unique personal experiences, so don't be alarmed I had to throw that disclaimer out there before we get started and you start reading.

So.....

Hit the lights Negro (line from *Boyz In Da Hood*) and play my theme music!

Every good hero should have one! (Line from *I'm Gonna Git You Sucka*)

THE EYE OF THE TIGER: THE ROCKY BALBOA SYNDROME (THE TRUE UNDERDOG)

"Rocky, Rocky, Rocky" The crowd shouts louder and louder. It's Sylvester Stallone's "spinach" as he gets stronger and stronger in the fight.

And then he does it. All bloody and weak. Rocky has done it again. Defeated the villain opponent that has haunted him the whole movie.

Man, I love *Rocky* movies and soundtrack- everything. All of them. Heck I can't wait for *Creed* to be release in November. If you aren't a Rocky movie buff, Creed takes place in Philadelphia in which Apollo Creed's son has become a boxer and seeks out Rocky to train him because he researched that Apollo and Rocky had some epic battles in the ring.

If you ask me, Rocky was the one who had Apollo's number and took his gold and his fans. He won the hearts of Philadelphia.

Even though I feel that the trials and struggles I've been through follow the same model of Job, the victories and the process follow Rocky and him having to overcome great odds to become victorious.

I've played a lot of sports in my life.

I've wrestled in high school, took up Brazilian Jut Jitsu, took up Muy Thai, took up training for a 5K and triathlon, played tennis, played soccer, basketball, tee-ball, and softball.

Of course football has been my bread and butter for many reasons.

For one, my momma and uncle loved it, and it gave me an opportunity to connect with the both of them. In little league Pop Warner football, I chose my football jersey number in honor of my uncle. Number 20. He played in high school but had to stop because his asthma was too bad causing complications. While all my friends were getting single digit numbers for their jersey. Each year I chose #20 for my Uncle Jerry. I made that number a legend during my time at the Greyhounds organization.

Two, my dad played the sport all the way up until college until he injured his shoulder and was forced into early retirement.

And three, it gave me a sense of identity throughout the early part of my life. I say even to this day it saved my life with the choices I made and stayed away from growing up in the environment I was in. People that knew me in my neighborhood and in school knew how much I loved football and how serious I took the game.

I later took up boxing when I was in grad school. I thought this would be a great opportunity to learn the sport and understand the grind that boxers have to go through to stand in the squared circle.

Boxing to me is a great real life metaphor and teacher. It taught me when I boxed and trained how to not throw in the towel when times get hard and tough. I can recall my first sparring match. That week, my coach repeatedly warned me to keep my hands up at all times to protect myself, but I would continue to drop them because my hands would get tired from holding them up. Those gloves started to feel like I was holding center-blocks in front of my face. So I would drop them. But because we were only using the focus mits and he was only tapping me to keep my hands up, I would drop them more times than I should have. All week he kept on me "keep your hands up", and all week I'll drop them. Well Saturday was Sparring Day so all we would do is spar. I had befriended a guy who I thought I definitely could take in the ring. I was twice his size as far as weight was concerned. Well I was painfully wrong. That little Mexican beat the Cowboy shit outta me. Every time I tried to land a punch, he was two or three steps ahead, around, and to either side of me. The lesson of keeping my hands up was painfully learned that day because he landed all his punches square to my face easily.

One thing about me, if I am losing in any competition, I internally place a goal in my head to at least accomplish something while going through the punishment. In football, if we were losing, and the opponent was a superior team, as long as they knew my presence on the field then I counted it as a moral victory. I wasn't considered one blessed with speed so where I wasn't blessed with speed I made up punishing the other guy. I needed to destroy you physically. Put my helmet through your spinal cord even if it caused damage to me in the process.

I'm not a tall guy. I joke and say I accidentally got in the wrong line when God was handing out height. But that didn't stop me on the field. I honestly thought I was just as tall as everyone else that was out there. It wasn't until I watched film one day and saw myself that I realized how short I really was in comparison to everyone else. I can remember the first time I saw myself and video. We were watching game film and I asked "who's that baby out there running around on the field?" They laughed and thought I was joking and teasing myself. They were like "that's you ". I couldn't believe it. In little league football, I played middle linebacker. In high school I played outside linebacker which meant I was taking on linemen twice my weight or height or most of the time both. So for me that was pretty darn impressive if you ask me.

Well back to the match, because "Speedy Gonzalez" was fast as grease lightning with everything he threw and his footwork was just amazing, I knew I didn't stack up to him in any area so I put a moral victory in my head as we went to our respective corners for advice and coaching. I remember as the coach was chewing me out I tuned him out and started giving myself advice. "Asim, he's too fast, too quick, he's too elusive so this is what we're gonna do. If you land one haymaker... one overhand right and stun him stop him in his tracks you've won the fight today regardless of what "Speedy" is doing out there. We came out from our corners touched gloves and began the round. Speedy was back at graciously giving me the opportunity of a lifetime wearing my face out. Then suddenly it happened. My opportunity for what seemed like a millisecond I landed my haymaker and stunned him. The other fighters went nuts. Heck I was even stunned. I didn't know what to do next because up until that point I was wearing leather like it was a normal thing. Speedy backed up and was dazed. But because I stunned him and didn't know what to do next, it gave him a moment to gather himself. Once he did, he went back to the blackboard to pick up where he had left off before the haymaker landed. I didn't care because I won morally.

When we finished the sparring session, he came over and gave me some pointers as to what I could work on as well as encouragement and compliments on the fight. He asked had I boxed before. I answer no that this was the first time and this week was my first week in the gym ever. I had never boxed anything other than my teddy bear after watching Rocky or playing Mike Tyson Punch Out on Nintendo. He said that though it was may first sparring session I did great for my first time in the ring.

I later found out that my sparring partner that day was an ex Intercontinental champion. The guys in the gym were amazed at how well I hung in there with him and how I went the distance.

I say all this to say that boxing taught me a valuable lesson on life. You can't run from life especially if you're faced with insurmountable obstacles. You may have family members, a husband or wife, kids, coworkers friends, neighbors, church members, your boss, just plain naysayers, doctors, lawyers, just people all around you shouting "you can't win Rocky!", but YOU have to know deep down inside that you can and have to WIN or else. Even if you get knock down you get back up. You have to put your mouthpiece back in and go at it again even harder, more determined, more focused. Even if you have to claw, scratch, crawl to the finish line. It doesn't matter how you do it. You just do it like Nike.

It's the Eye of the Tiger!

Allow me to Reintroduce Myself

I've been through a lot during the 37 years on this Earth. Some good. Some bad. Some scary. Some funny. Some dark. God doesn't I feel operate through chances, luck, or coincidences. **But** what He has done in, my life, is work through and on me.

Those that know me know I try to bring laughter to whatever the situation that's happening to or around me. Some may think that some things are serious life changing moments. They should warrant a 'stone face' approach. I, on the contrary, feel nothing in life is 'too serious'. I feel that the best comedians are the ones who can make you laugh at their own pain. Richard Pryor, Mike Epps, Kevin Hart. So the experiences that I share in this book I try to get those who I'm sharing this story with to laugh with me at the things that God has brought me through.

MIAMI VICE AND THE FIRST TIME

Friday night in October 1984.

I remember it like it was yesterday. My older sister was in her room sleep like always. My mom had just got off work, and my grandma was in her room. Her oxygen machine was on and you could smell that stale hospital smell coming out the room. It was passed my bedtime but because my momma went into her room to check on her she didn't say anything to me. *Miami Vice* was just coming on. I loved that show. It was about a little after 11:30 because the local news had just went off. I was laying on the living room floor coloring in one of my fairy tale coloring books. I loved to color back then. I was coloring in the Jack in the Beanstalk coloring book and I overheard my momma and grandma talking about my uncle coming by earlier that day and he and her having a discussion on how he wanted to put her in a nursing home because the cancer was taking a toil on her health and she really didn't have anyone who could sit with her during the day until my momma got off work. My momma was trying to calm her down and reassure her that no one was going to put her in a nursing home.

Then I came up in the conversation. My momma was talking about my coloring books and my grandma was worried about how I would sometimes get mad when the crayons would break and she didn't want to have to deal with me and my tantrums. My momma reassured her again that if she had any problems out of me that when my momma got off work to tell her and she definitely would deal with me and it. I was like "hey, how did I get in the conversation with beatings?" I needed for them to keep me out of their conversation. Then all of a sudden it got quiet. Real quiet. The only thing that could be heard going was the oxygen machine. I stopped coloring and made my way towards my grandma room. Before I could go in to see what was going on, my momma stopped me and took me to her room. I stood on the box spring at the edge of her bed and she said "momma's dead" and she started crying. Me being only knee high to a horsefly just hugged her. I was 6 at the time so what did I know about giving someone comfort. Heck I had just recently learned how to tie my own shoes and "wrap my own ass". I remembered as I was hugging her a voice inside my head said "YOU WILL BE AT YOUR MOTHER'S DEATH BED" I remember how after about 10 minutes, she got herself together dried her face and proceeded to call relatives, friends, and her siblings to inform them grandma was no longer with us. I watched as she was so calm with each phone call. She would hang up and go to the next caller. As people started coming over and the ambulance came it was like she was so calm cool and collected.

But that was Yvette. Never let them see you sweat. Just get it done period.

I watched the whole thing unfold. I even slipped into grandma's room while momma and the EMT were talking. They asked her questions about how grandma died. I can recall one of them tell her she shouldn't have cut the oxygen machine off until after they had arrived because that could have been grounds for suspicious foul play. I remember my momma telling them she didn't know. She thought since grandma was died, the machine didn't need to stay on. Again, I watched it all. By this time my older sister had just got up in which I was like you have missed all the excitement. Family members continued to come and momma never ever shed one single tear the whole time people were there. Her voice was calm as she retold the last moments with grandma.

Mae, one of the funniest people you ever wanted to meet. Adamant wrestling fan. Loved Dusty Rhodes. Hated Ric Flair, but you better not interrupt her when wrestling was on. Her best friend would come over sometimes to watch it with her. They'd be in hollering, screaming, yelling, and laughing all at the same time at the tv like they were at the matches live.

The NWA on TBS Saturday evenings at 6p.

She would say wrestling was real. Football was fake. Grown men in tight pants grabbing each other to the ground and jumping on each other. It was just plain dumb and didn't make sense.

The first time I met my dad was at my grandma's funeral. It was night time and my momma took me into the foyer and there he was standing there. I remember running up to him and jumping into his arms. He took me outside where he had a van similar to the A Team; CB radio, tented windows, and all. He put me in the driver seat where I pretended like I was driving. Man, one thing I remember most about him was he always smelled good his cologne left a scent on your clothes and on your hands, and he had great muscle.

He came about two or three more times and then like *Keyser Soza*, from *The Usual Suspects*, **poof** he was gone.

THE BIRTH OF MY THUNDER BUDDY & DIE HARD 1: THE FIRST ATTEMPT ON MY LIFE

Saturday, August 16, 1987 11pm as we were driving back from seeing my baby sister being born from the previous night we, my cousins, older sister, and I left the hospital, I went to sleep in the backseat with my cousin, her brother. My cousin was driving her Chevette. She later explained to me that it had been raining off and on, we were going through a caution "yellow" light when another car ran their caution "red" light and because they couldn't stop, they slammed into us causing us to spin uncontrollably into someone's front yard. I was the only one to suffer injuries. I sustained a broken right knuckle that was in two pieces and a major cut to my left cheek in which I had to receive stitches. I remember waking to everyone crying so I started to join in. When in Rome do what the Romans do right? I didn't know why we were crying. At that time I didn't even notice that I had broken anything or was injured in the first place. I just heard everyone crying so I started crying. I didn't want to be the only one with "the dry face" left out. I remember my sister holding me a crying uncontrollably. She had on a yellow polo shirt but it was red which I later realized it was from my blood. She was rocking me back and forth and crying.

I remember in the ambulance having to stay up and repeat answers to questions from the attendant.

"What's your full name?"

Asim Suah Khalfani

"How old are you?"

8 but will be 9 next month

When were you born?

September 14, 1978

"Where do you live?"

1229 Free Street (remember that number you gonna see it again), Winston-Salem, NC 28127

"Where are you?"

In an ambulance

"Do you know where you are and where you're going?"

In an ambulance going to the hospital

"What's your full name?"

Asim Suah Khalfani

"How old are you?"

8 going on 9

"Where are you?"

In an ambulance

"Where are we headed?"

The hospital

All I wanted to do is go back to sleep and for him to just wake me up once we got to the hospital ER. I kept asking him repeatedly since he was asking me the same questions over and over "can I go back to sleep?" Occasionally I would throw in a "Please" to soften the question hoping it would change his response but it didn't. I started to get irritated because I just couldn't understand why this guy was forgetting the answers I was giving him to the same questions that he kept asking over and over like a broken record. I also remember him asking me one time were there any other place I was injured or hurt and I had to drop my pants so he could examine me. Again I was half asleep and just wanted to go back to sleep period. So I did what he asked. It was then I noticed the displaced knuckle when I tried to pull my pants down.

When we got to the hospital I remember going in the back and the doctor playing the game 'Operation' with my hand in which I yelled at him and said a profanity.

Oopsie! Did I say that?

I thought it was appropriate because he could see that the knuckle was in two pieces and one of the pieces was down the middle of my hand. He didn't have to touch it. And to ask does this hurt?

What do you think Captain Obvious?

I remember they set it back in place, casted it up and then laid me on the table to begin putting stitches in my face. They put a white towel over my entire face and a square was cut out just big enough for them to do the stitch operation.

I remember before the doctor started asking me did I want the removable kind or a new kind of stitches that dissolved on its own. Based on how much pain I was in with the broken knuckle I elected to go with the dissolvable ones because I didn't want to have to come back so that they would have to remove them later.

As they begin stitching my face, I remember it hurting so bad that I tried to lie and say I couldn't breath underneath the towel, that the towel was obstructing my airway, but they knew that I was lying and only trying to get them to stop. All of the doctors kept saying "we're almost finish just a little bit more", but I wasn't buying that brand. I just wanted them to stop so my sister and I could leave and go to my momma's friend apartment. Besides, we were scheduled to go swimming the next day so I needed my rest. I knew it was late and all I wanted to do is go back to sleep and get out of the hospital. When he was done I remember the doctor giving me detailed instructions as well as to my older sister and cousin that I had to stay away from water because of the cast and the stitches. Well there goes me going to the swimming pool since that was on the itinerary. But I was so sleepy and in pain from the knuckle and stitches that I failed to noticed that my bottom lip was swollen and I had minor cuts on the inside of my lower lip which prevented me eating any solid foods. I didn't find that out until later that morning when I woke up to eat some sour cream potato chips and the salt burned my cuts in my lip. So for two weeks all I ate was ice cream and tomato soup because that was the only thing that didn't aggravate the cuts inside my lower lip. I got tired of both ice cream and tomato soup by the beginning of week three and never picked them up again until 2006. By the time school started back I had a brand new cast on my hand and stitches in my face. I had to regurgitate how I ended up with it and the mark on my face when we had to tell what we did over the summer for the first couple of weeks back in school. Most people talked about how they spent their summer on vacation traveling to different states. When it came my turn all I had to do is stand and the audience could see what I did over the summer.

Keyser Sosa aka my dad came over again. I looked a hot mess and I can recall running back and forth to the bathroom to check my face because my lip was still swollen and my face was still scarred up. I felt embarrassed looking the way I did. He stayed for about two hours and left. Then Keyser Soza disappeared yet again. I wouldn't reconnect back up with him until September 2005, but this time it would be through he and I writing each other while he was in prison.

Are We There Yet?-Die Hard 2:The Second Attempt on My Life

I was in the 7th grade. My mom, little sister, and I were headed to my Pop Warner football game. We were headed down the street traveling southbound when this big city dump Mack truck like the ones that come in your neighborhood to cut down tree limbs was at the intersection. But instead of them stopping because we had the right away, they proceeded to go through the stop sign. They hit us so hard that our car's impact cut through the stop sign bending and knocking it completely over. The EMT unit had to use the "jaws of life" to cut my mom out of the car because she was pinned in. My little sister and I immediately got out the car through the back seat. I remember thinking "on movies cars always exploded from taking an impact such as the one we had just experienced". So my initial thought was grab my sister and get the hell outta there!

Somebody had to survive to tell the story right? Hey somebody needed to be around just in case the news crew needed to interview someone to get the story.

Why not me? Right?

Once EMT workers got my mom out and we got to the hospital, because everything happened so fast it wasn't until then in the ER that I realized this was the first time I was going miss my game. We were playing the King Dolphins. They were pretty sorry and I had calculated that I probably could have scored at least four or five times to catch my best friend in our touchdown challenge that he and I had placed at the beginning of our season. I can remember sitting thinking I wish I could get in contact with my coach to see if anyone could come and pick me up at the hospital before the game started. I mean I still could play and I was semi dressed out.

That's how I've always been. Steady and focus on the task at hand. I remember my coach saying "Asim Suah Khalfani is like a heat seeking missile. Once he's locked in on something it's a done deal". Well it's safe to say I missed that game and my best friend scored about five or six times that day. When I called him when we got back home, he made sure I knew how many he scored. It wasn't any way now I was going to close in on our little competition with me missing that game because our next two opponents were stiff competition-the Tiny Indians and then the Tiny Vikings. We would face the Vikings in the playoffs to see who would go to the Sertoma Bowl. We lost to them and we didn't make it to the Sertoma Bowl. That was the first time my mom missed the remaining of my games but it wouldn't be the last time sad to say.

The EMT and doctors said that with the way the car had been totaled from the accident that we were lucky to have survived the accident with how big the truck was in comparison to how small our Hyundai Civic was. To have taken that type of impact from the truck was a miracle. No one should have made it out of an accident such as that.

The only person who received injuries was my momma. She had some cracked ribs and a collapsed lung. But did that stop Yvette from going to work the following week?

No.

She made arrangements to get rides to work and she was back on her job cracked ribs and all by the middle of the week. That's how she operated. We don't quit. We may slow down to catch our breath but stop.... NEVER!

She also made provisions to get me to practices and games because she didn't want me to miss any more games for the rest of the season. She knew how important football was to me and how much it brought me joy.

Boyz In Da Hood

Now Happy Hill Gardens to some who didn't live over in the neighborhood was one of the worst places to raise a family. If you were a young black male growing up over in the Gardens you were expected to either become a drug dealer or be involved in some type of illegal activity. You were expected to have been arrested by the time you turn 18th at least once. Majority of the mothers over there were expected to be on welfare and living off the government.

I, on the other hand, never saw "the Gardens" as outsiders did. We were a tight knit group of people who came together when it mattered the most.

Granted gun shots at night were the norm. I could remember at night hearing them, but that didn't bother me. I felt safe when I went to sleep. Hearing it was what I considered my "Ghetto lullaby", you got use to it. It was like a person who lived in the country hearing the sounds of crickets at night. Heck I would get worried anytime I didn't hear gunshots at night because that wasn't normal.

I had guns pulled out on me, been shot at, as well as been around gun play several times while living over there, but God kept me safe and secure. I've stared down the barrel of guns looking at the bullet so to speak on at least 3 separate occasions.

The first time was on the school bus my 7th grade year in middle school. The guy sitting in the seat with me pulled it on me and threatened to use it on me if I told the assistant principal and it got back that I was the one who snitched him out.

My response. "Heck I can't stand her. She gets on my nerves. I don't talk to her anyway; she's too nosey".

We got off the bus and he went his way and I went mine like nothing happened.

The second incident was the summer of my 8th and 9th grade year. I use to hang out with my next door neighbor a lot during my 8th and 9th grade. One day at the gas station before we went to play basketball, I was waiting for him to come back from paying for the gas. I took out his revolver from the glove compartment and started playing with it. When he got back in the car from paying for the gas, he ask me why I was playing with his gun and to hand him it. I did and he pointed the gun right at me. Point blank range. He looked at me and ask me what was I going to do. I told him don't ever point that at me unless he intended on using it and if I was on the receiving end that he better make sure that he killed me because if I got the chance to repay the favor I was going to make sure he wouldn't have to worry about me missing the opportunity and messing up. He laughed at me and said I was crazy and he was just playing and for me to put the gun back in the glove compartment where I got it from. But I told him I wasn't playing that if he ever pull that stunt on me again we would have a problem. We went on to go and play basketball and it never got mentioned again.

On a third occasion, our football team was at a summer passing league when one of my teammates thought it would be cool to bring his 9 millimeter on the trip with us. I guess he thought we needed his "top flight security" tactics if a gangster hijacked the activity bus on our way down there or something. I call him 2 cents-a mixture of the rappers 2pac & 50 cents. My thought process was different. I was worried that the head coach could catch him with the gun and that we all would get in deep trouble and be subject to running suicides after practice until the cows came home. So I told him he was stupid for bringing it. It must have upset him because he pointed it straight at me. I told him calmly never pull a gun out on someone unless you plan to use it. His response was something along the lines of that I thought I was so tough. I reiterated again never pull a gun on someone unless you intended to use it. I went to my seat, sat down, and we all went our merry way.

Now I've also had the "pleasure" of being shot at and around gun play.

One day while on the basketball court a guy came on the court and started shooting in the air. Now I can remember yelling at myself internally that I should have gone home earlier when I had the chance. Instead, now I'm caught in this mess dealing with this. No I wanted to get that last game in before the street lights came on. I sat down and waited for him to leave before I ran home. I got home and washed up for dinner, sat down, and ate like it was a normal day.

Remember the guy who pulled the gun out on me before school had started? Well he's back.

This time my friend and I was playing outside and my friend thought it would be funny to pick on him. He, on the other hand, didn't think the jokes were funny and decided to shot at us. While we ran off my friend still continued to pick at him as he shot at us. We laughed all the way home. It still was funny the things he was calling him.

Big fat funky nasty

It's still funny til this day.

Another occasion my friends and I were waiting on the activity bus for summer workouts for football when this notorious drug dealer in the neighborhood came stood in the middle of the street pulled out his Nickel plated 9 millimeter and proceeded to shoot up the street at a porch full of guys who were sitting outside. Once he shot at them he ran off laughing. He ran one way we ran the opposite. I ventured to say I missed that session that day. I got back home and played my Super Nintendo for the rest of the day until it was time to eat dinner.

I wrote this chapter not to brag but to demonstrate how God was my protector and my shield through all of those life threatening episodes.

Some of my friends weren't so lucky. One in particular shot himself in the head on accident playing with a gun.

Another incident, a guy got shot and he became paralyzed for life. G had another plan for how my life would end and I thank Him.

THE FAMILY VACATION

I remember the summer of 1994, my mother, sisters, next door neighbor, and I went to Carowinds amusement park. It was hot like August usually is. My next door neighbor, my older sister, and I was boarding Thunder Road roller coaster while my momma elected to sit this one out with my younger sister. As we got on the roller coaster, I looked down and my momma was bent over and she had to sit down on the wall next to the ride. I was worried because that wasn't normal. My little sister looked worried too. We got through the ride and I immediately ran over to ask her what was wrong. Why were she sitting over there and why was she bent over a moment ago?

She said she was just tired from all the heat and standing in line but it wasn't anything to be concerned with and were we ready to go home because we had pretty much been there for all day. Everyone except me was ok with deciding to leave. I not only wanted to stay, but I wanted to know why all of a sudden she was too tired and too hot to keep going.

I remembered as we were walking back to the car I kept a close eye on her and repeatedly asked was she ok. When we got back home she just sat on the couch. She said she had to "get herself together" because she was tired from all the walking and standing in line.

Later that night I still checked on her periodically because that wasn't typical Yvette behavior. By the end of the month, momma would come home from work and just go straight to bed. Before she would go in her room, she'd ask if we wanted her to cook otherwise she felt tired from working all day and needed to go to bed. I was a sophomore in high school. Even though I thought I was ready to master the kitchen, she didn't, so I was left with Doritos and/or Pork n Beans, microwave hamburgers, boiled smoke sausage links, or scrambled eggs sandwiches with fried bologna.

That's what my younger sister had too. Hey when in Rome, EAT what the Romans eat.

Some nights she wouldn't even take her uniform off she would just collapse on the bed and fall asleep. The sleepy behavior got worst to the point she started losing massive amounts of weight. Her uniform from work hung off her body and she just looked thin.

FRIDAY NIGHT LIGHTS

The symptoms didn't get any better they only got worst. One night after I came home from my football game, she called me into her room. She asked if I could call 911. She needed to go to the hospital. I was scared.

Why she'd needed to call the ambulance?

Why she'd needed to go to the hospital?

Anytime those two words were together in the same sentence something seriously was wrong. The last time an ambulance came to **1229** my younger sister was born in '87 and I knew she wasn't having any relations let alone pregnant.

But now wasn't the time for 21 questions.

I called and as we waited for them to arrive, she told me to call my uncle so she could see if he could make arrangements to take me and my younger sister over to her friend's house while she was in the hospital because she didn't want us to be there alone by ourselves. My younger sister and I got along great so it wasn't an issue of us fighting at all like my older sister and I growing up. Her and I always were fighting and bickering/bothering each other. More so, she thought she was the boss and I was the servant.

My younger sister and I, on the other hand, were more like partners in crime. Things got broke. No one knew who was responsible even if we both would get in trouble unlike my older sister, she couldn't wait to snitch me out at a drop of a dime. So my uncle came and got us as the ambulance took my mother to the hospital. We packed a few things and left. Little did we know she would be in the hospital for 6-8 months.

I never went to visit her during any of the times she ever stayed in the hospital. I don't do hospitals. I hate the smell and it reeks of death looming.

Besides it reminded me of how grandma's room smelt when she got sick when I was 6.

Naw I'll pass. I'll just wait until you come back home.

When she was released she looked really thin and she needed a walker to get around. The doctors had diagnosed her with Lupus.

What they hell is Lupus?

It really messed with my psyche because I was use to the Yvette that didn't need a walker. The Yvette who came home from work and cooked us dinner. The Yvette who came to my football games. Heck the last and final game she came to see me play in was my first high school football game. I played junior varsity that year, and we were playing East Forsyth. We lost on a muff punt in which our punter kicked the ball in the butt of the center. We fumbled it, they recovered, and scored.

She never saw me play in another game again.

She had gotten so sick during her first stay, the medical team thought she wouldn't make it out and die. But remember that's not the "Our way", Yvette fought back to the point that she was released from the hospital. God had another part to the manuscript.

She had missed my whole sophomore year of high school and I was now heading into my junior year. She didn't get to see me play my first year of varsity as a sophomore but it was ok. She was home now. Not like the old days before she got Lupus, but she was home.

My junior year she went in the hospital about two or three more times during that school year. I can recall asking her could I stay home instead of going back over with my younger sister to her friend's house. She agreed and I stayed home. Besides I now had a job so I would go after school to weight training and go to work. My high school coach would drop me off. I would have to catch the bus coming back. Now this is where it gets crazy. The bus schedule was crazy because the bus wouldn't come out there until 10:45 and it ran every 45 minutes until midnight. I would get off work at 10 pm wait 45 minutes and get to the bus station downtown around 11:45-midnight. Get on my bus that would head to my neighborhood around 1:45. Get off at my stop around 2 am and get home. I would do my homework if I had some at work (if any of you reading were wondering) take a shower and be in bed by 2:30 am.

I would have to get up around 6-6:15am to get ready for school, cook my breakfast (yeah I was cooking now! Who's gonna stop me? I gotta eat) and catch the school bus by 730am. This went on for the remainder of my high school career when she would have to go in and stay in the hospital.

Nobody ever knew because that's the "Our way". We don't gripe or complain we just get stuff done period. Momma was in and out of the hospital the remaining time I was in high school.

YOU GONNA EAT YO CORNBREAD?

One time momma had got out the hospital and I wanted to surprise her with a complete meal I had learned how to cook. It was the first meal that I learned on my own. This is what we put at the Cafe:

Hamburger Helper Oriental

Jiffy cornbread

Red Kool-Aid

She was ecstatic. Here her son was fixing her a real meal. It beat the Pork n Beans and smoke sausage links on Wonder Bread. Little did she know I had been eating Hamburger Helper Oriental for 2 weeks straight with Jiffy cornbread.

I had became a pro at making Jiffy cornbread.

1/3 milk

1 egg

Mix and put in the oven at 425. Yep what?

She ate all of it and even asked for seconds. What? Now she was showing out. I was planning to take the leftovers for lunch/dinner for work the next day, but I didn't mind too much.

We ate and she loved it. I told her she wouldn't hurt my feelings to be honest. She said she loved it. She said it was great and that it was the first time eating that version of Hamburger Helper. She suggested if I liked, she would show me some other things that I could make. Wow the master chef sharing with the student her knowledge. She also wanting to know if I could take on the cooking duties for my younger sister and I.

Heck yeah. You ain't said nothing. I would love the opportunity.

So the baton was passed and that's when I took over the kitchen and cooking duties.

I'M A SURVIVOR

My senior year of high school it was routine for momma to go into the hospital and stay for a couple of weeks so it didn't bother me as much. I had survived the toughest years of my life. My whole thought process throughout the 3 years she was sick and in and out of the hospital was please God don't have them call me to the main office to tell me "we're sorry to inform you your mother is dead".

So I survived. Heck yeah. Most kids my age during that time was thinking about non serious things like the prom, getting a car maybe, relationship woos, whether they had enough credits to graduate. I, on the other hand, was thinking about will I have to be a professional drug dealer if momma dies? This thought never left me. I always thought about it 24/7 and had a neighborhood drug dealer's pager number in my head on speed dial just in case I got the news she was dead. He would stop by occasionally to check up on me and play video games with me. Little did I know, he was only keeping me close to him because he was trying to leer me into the streets and on the block to work for him selling drugs. That was later confirmed and told to me by him when my mother had passed, and he was high on marijuana and loose with his lips so to speak.

Anyway we survived. She was alive. I was graduating and going off to college in the fall. Things were starting to look on the up and up. My high school was having its annual seniors awards ceremony in the gymnasium. It was there that my classmates saw my mother for the first time and it was revealed she was sick. Momma had lost her hair from Lupus and her skin had lesions, she was still thin and looked frail, but so what. My Queen was there to support her prince and I wanted her to see how hard I had been working through this most difficult time. I got so many awards that day.

Here's the awards I won:

Graduated with perfect attendance all 4 years

National Honor Society member

Who's Who Among High School students

Varsity letterman 3 years in football

Varsity letterman in wrestling 2 years

3.6 GPA

Top 20 percentile among the high school students in my graduating class

Academic scholarship to a private university

Awarded a scholarship from a NFL football player who grew up in the Winston-Salem Housing Authorities

It seem like every time I came up to receive an award and return to my seat, they were calling me up there again to get another award.

I felt great not because of all the attention, but because my mother was in the audience and got to witness her baby boy's hard work and dedication had paid off. To me that was the biggest award I could have received that day. Inspite of all we had been through, the scares, the sacrifices, the hospital stays away from her family, and long hours coming home from work after going to school all day, working out, and then going to work for 4-6 hours, WE DID IT!

She fought.

I stayed focused and God kept us both.

Thank you Jesus! We couldn't have done none of it without you.

The Magician

In addition to all of that, I had the opportunity to be featured in the city's newspaper, The Winston-Salem Journal. I was scheduled to be featured on the front page. It talked about how I grew up in a bad neighborhood but stayed focus inspite of the environment I was in.

I remember the reporter asking me how did I do it, maintain such focus regardless of the fact so many around me wasn't and didn't?

My response was simple. My mother taught me it's not where you start but where you finish. Your present circumstances doesn't necessarily mean it's your final destination. I never once thought this was the end of my journey. I knew I would be going on to bigger and better things.

A couple of months later the interview was published.

This part was later told to me by my older sister because I was off at college when the article was published.

My sister said it was a Sunday morning and they were in the kitchen when they heard a knock at the door. My sister asked was momma expecting someone. She said no and told her to go see who it was. She went but there was no one standing outside the door. She went back in the kitchen with momma. Another knock was at the door, then the door bell rang. Then another and another. When her and momma both went outside to catch the culprit who they thought was playing on the door, they found all these newspapers laying on the front porch. On the front page was a picture of me. The article that the reporter had interviewed me had been published. My sister said my mom broke down and start crying. She said "My baby finally did it. He finally made it".

Correction momma "**you did it**". Your hard work and tenacious spirit and valuable lessons that groomed me and molded me did it. You put in those tireless hours and it now had paid off a thousandfold. That was all your doing. The magician's magic was revealed to the whole city that

Sunday morning. Readers got a glimpse of how awesome a job the selfish less sacrifice, hard work, and dedication to making me want nothing but the best had paid off.

Proverbs says *a wise son brings joy to his father (mother), but a foolish man despises his mother* Proverbs 15:20 NIV.

Your secret was no more. It was public!

RUNNING OUT OF TIME

My sophomore year had started in college. My goal was to be in the starting lineup on the football team, and I did, as well as, the previous spring semester, I was awarded athletic scholarship money for performing well during Spring Ball.

Goal accomplished!

For some odd reason though I was having this urge to get home. The Christmas break couldn't get here fast enough. When I got home, I was so excited to just be home spending every waking hour around my momma. I remember when she came to pick me up from school, I told her that she would be proud of me because I knew I had gotten a 4.0 (ALL A's) which was a first for my college career. When the mail came a couple of weeks later, it was confirmed.

President's List 4.0

I as well as she was ecstatic. A 4.0. I had made all A's many times in my scholastic career, but college. Who would have imagine it?

She still was moving around gingerly like she sometimes did. So I didn't think nothing of it. All 3 of her kids were under the same roof. My older sister had come down from Charlotte, my younger sister was there being her usual self which was just being happy that her older two siblings were home together. So that for me was the greatest Christmas present I could have asked for.

We would spend time just laughing and watching tv and old VCR movies. My older sister and I was getting along quite well. No arguments. No disagreements. No fighting.

Now that was a first. We were having just a Huxable type of experience without Cliff.

I remember coming back from the gym from doing one of the Christmas break workouts we had been assigned to do over break. As I was coming into the neighborhood, my older sister and momma was leaving out. They spotted me and I them. We exchange a couple of words and my sister said they would be back shortly. I didn't think nothing of it. They pulled off in one direction and I the other.

It was later explained to me that momma wanted to go to the hospital, but she didn't want my sister to say anything to me when they left.

At the hospital, momma wanted them to keep her. My sister said when the doctor told her that there was nothing else they could do, momma yelled at him.

My sister said she quickly told her to calm down and why was she yelling. Momma looked away. My sister said a tear ran down momma's cheek. They left and came back home.

THE MONOPOLY LESSON

We decided one night to play Monopoly. My momma never liked to play Monopoly. She thought the game took too long. She was more of an Uno/ Phase 10 type of person, but this particular time she wanted to play.

We played and laughed for hours. All of us played, my two sisters, my momma, and me. My momma though she never liked the game was killing all of us. She collected more properties than all 3 of us combined. She got tired and wanted to stop.

Before she stopped, I thought I should be the one who got her properties and money. Of course my older sister thought she should. My younger sister was acting like she always did. All she wanted was for us all to get along like Rodney King.

My momma thought otherwise and disagreed with us both. She said "I'm tired now, so before I go I'm going to divide all my properties and money among the three of y'all. Is that a deal? And y'all can keep playing if you want."

I still tried to weasel my way into letting me be in charge of dividing the money and properties among us three. Of course my younger sister and I would get more than my older sister. Momma won't agree to that proposal. She started counting out the money she had into threes. Anything that couldn't be equally distributed, the bank received it. Once she was finished with her money the properties then were divided equally. All houses and hotels went back to the bank. When she was done she got up and went into her room.

Damn Yvette you were so smart. It wouldn't be to years later when I got alone that I understood what you were doing. The final lesson before the final exam. No pop quizzes here. Put all study materials away. She was prepping us for what was lurking in the bushes.

Christmas came I didn't get much and I didn't want much. Again I was content with being by my momma.

THE QUIET BEFORE THE STORM

My middle school best friend wanted me to come over to visit with him, my high school ex girlfriend that we both knew from middle school, and his ex girlfriend that he dated in middle school. I really didn't want to go. I wanted to spend every waking hour with momma, but she insisted. She wanted me to go and spend some time with my friends since we all was in town. So because she wanted me to, I went. I stayed over there until the early hours of the morning laughing, joking, and reminiscing about middle school, middle school teachers that people talked about, and classmates. I got home went to bed because I had to be at work in a couple of hours.

1229

Job experience #1

I woke to find that it was starting to snow, but it wasn't sticking so I went in to work. Besides momma wasn't big on staying out of work because of the weather. She advised me to take my time when I was on the road and it wasn't bad to begin with out there. I left and told her I would be back before it got bad anyway. She agreed and said she had been looking at the news and they said it wasn't going to get bad until I got off work anyway.

When I got home she was sitting in the living room watching *Price Is Right*. By that time the snow was coming down and it was sticking and accumulating. She ask me if I could go back out to pay the car insurance bill. I told her it was starting to look bad out there and I didn't think it was possible. Her vibe felt strange for some reason. I told her I was going to lie down and catch a nap since I didn't get in until early that morning.

Before I left to go in her room I ask if there was anything she needed. She again asked if I could go and pay the car insurance. I told her that was out of the question. That request wasn't happening with how bad it was starting to look. She said ok and I left to go in her room. Growing up, I loved sleeping in her bed and smelling the pillow case she laid on. So I went in her room. I was awaken to hear a thud sound. It was her trying to walk down the hallway to her room. I got up and yelled at her because she scared me.

Now I was the only one there with her so I had to make sure everything was alright and she was ok. My older sister had traveled back to Charlotte to beat the snow storm, and my younger sister had went to spend the night with some friends. So it was me and her.

I yelled at her that she should've called for me to help her to her bedroom instead of trying to do it herself. But that was Yvette. Never quit never surrender do it yourself. I helped her to the bed and told her in a jokingly manner, "momma you got a college football player here if need be I'll carry you to the bedroom. I asked one more time before I went out to the living room was it anything else she needed. She answered "can you go pay the car insurance?" Before I walked out I looked her dead in her eyes and she looked back at me as if to say "I'm tired, can I go?" I nodded my head slightly to say "yes" and walked out the room.

It wasn't no more than about ten or fifteen minutes, I called back to see if she was ok and needed anything but there was no response. I called back there again no response still. I walked back to her room to find her face down in her vomit gasping for air. I immediately call 911 though it was an emergency situation I was calm. I stood by her window to watch for the ambulance. I never once freaked out even when they got there. They put her on the stretcher and I grabbed my coat and her Medicad card. We got in the ambulance but I started picking up signs that this wasn't good. When I was younger, my grandma and momma use to say if they don't turn the sirens on when they're speeding out the neighborhood then whoever they are transporting is probably already dead. Well they never turn the sirens on as we were rushing out the neighborhood to the hospital. **Sign #1**

On the way there, the attendant in the back who was with her beat on the glass for the driver to pull off to the side of the road to come in the back to help. When he got out it still was snowing and cold, and he wasn't breathing hard or sweating. When he returned, he was drenched in sweat and breathing like he had just came from the gym from a vicious workout. **Sign #2**

When we pulled up to the ER and the doctors ran out to meet them, before I got out I asked the driver calmly "is she gonna make it?"

He said "no, it doesn't look good. It looks bad. I don't think so".

I thanked him and closed his door and walked to check us in at the desk and waited in the waiting room until the doctors came and got me. I was calm and had a peace that I've never received nor ever experienced ever again. The doctors eventually came and took me in the back to a room.

The male doctor was making comments about my college jacket I had on as we walked in the room. This was a serious matter, and he was concern with my college coat I had on. **Sign #3**

Then he proceeded to talk in past tense verbs like we worked, she fought, we tried. **Sign #4**

Before he could tell me she was gone I had figured it out and started crying. They said they were sorry for the lost and they wanted to take me to where she was to view the body. My uncle was in the process of trying to get there but didn't arrive until after I had viewed her body.

There she was Yvette laying there on the table with a bronchial tube still stuck in her mouth. I immediately yelled out "get that FUCKING tube out her mouth. That ain't my momma". She looked as if she was in so much pain lying there. By that time my uncle had arrived, he grabbed me and told me to come on. It was going to be ok.

As he was taking me back home all I could think about was our last real conversation her and I had earlier that day and how all she was concern with was me going out to pay the car insurance bill. Not I love you or I always have been proud of you. No she was concern with me paying a damn car insurance bill.

When I got back home I walked to her bedroom. Her gown and slippers were still on the bed as if they were waiting for her to put them on. Then all of a sudden I remembered that voice when I was 6 "YOU WILL BE AT YOUR MOTHER'S DEATH BED", I broke down and started crying. Who would have thought 13 years later it would come true.

After getting myself together I did exactly what momma did when grandma died. I got on the phone and started calling her siblings, relatives, and friends.

Damn the same house that grandma died in those same people were coming back to meet up again. Just as she was calm so was I. Just like she didn't shed any tears while people were over nor did I. I had a great teacher and a great role model to imitate.

Yvette born June 30, 1953
died December 29, 1997
12/29 the same address number we resided **1229** Free Street.

I can remember going back in the back where she would show me as a little boy time and time again where the life insurance policy was located and her instructions *"when you go in the funeral home don't be up in there crying because the funeral director will rob you blind off emotions. If you need to cry, cry before you get there or after you leave.*

Also don't put my glasses on me when I'm laying in that casket. People look crazy laying in a casket dead with glasses on. You don't wear your glasses when you sleep so why put them on when you're dead. Just plain stupid.

Don't put any jewelry on me. The grave diggers ain't gonna do nothing but take it off me before they drop me into the ground.

When they close the casket DO NOT open it up again. When you close it keep it close.

Also no flowers. I hated flowers when I was living so it's no use to being there when I'm dead and gone".

It's funny how quickly your life can be altered- one minute your life is normal. The next minute you don't even know if you're coming or going. I woke up with a mother and us living in my childhood apartment. Now as I was going to sleep no mother and a lot of unanswered questions.

Wow. What's next?

Everything she requested the Queen got. I did all the funeral arrangements myself because it was my honor and duty.

When we rode to the funeral my great aunt said something that has stuck with me til today. She said that sometimes God chooses to pluck roses out His garden when they have matured and fully bloomed. She said my momma had served her purpose. Even though all of us were still young, He knew we would be alright. On the way to the church, a homeless guy was on the side of the road, he stood up, took his hat off to pay his respects as we rode down the street.

Wow!

When we got to the church I saw how many people had come out to pay their last respects to my mother sitting in the sanctuary. I didn't know she had touched so many lives in the short 44 years she was on this earth.

I can recall at the start of service, I was cracking jokes picking on what people had on at her funeral. It wasn't until the pallbearer pushed her casket down the aisle that I broke down and started crying. I think it was him wheeling her down the aisle which made me realize that it was real and final.

We buried her and three weeks later I was back in school for the spring semester. I stayed in school the rest of the time. Yvette won't allow me to quit. She won't allow that. So I went back.

When my roommates asked me "what You do over the Christmas break?"

My response was bury my momma.

I remember one of them ask me why you back?

My response was where else am I going to go?

I ended up finishing and receiving a bachelor of science degree in athletic training. Here are my collegiate awards that I obtained:

Graduated Cum Laude honor

3.6 GPA

Who's Who Among Colleges and Universities

First to ever complete the athletic training program and play football simultaneously

Phi Eta Sigma national honor society member

Academic All American in football

1 of 5 to charter a historical black fraternity on a predominantly white campus. Then I went on to purse and receive a masters of science degree in kinesiology and recreation.

Before I go from this chapter, I would be crazy not to mention all of this all of the things that I experienced during momma's sickness and death is not a pride thing; me boasting about look at what I did. Remember in Jeremiah it talks about how He knew me before I was even in my mother's womb so all of the accomplishments and accolades that I accumulated during those 6-8 years was God. He gets all the praise, honor, and glory. He kept and carried me and still is.

SWEET DREAMS ARE MADE OF THESE

One night after momma's death when I was back in school, I had this strange dream, but it seemed so real.

I was in my high school weight room. I was doing incline bench and my outside linebacker coach was standing over me spotting me as I lift the weights on the bar.

When I was done doing my set, I sat up and look at the clock. Then all of a sudden I was in the hallway and it was filled with nothing but girls. I walked down the hallway and they were everywhere. Numerous. So many they were on top of each other. I continued down the hallway and then something told me to look back. When I did two girls were kissing and one started eating the face of the other until it was just one girl standing there. Then I started throwing fireballs from my hands towards her and shouting "I REBUKE YOU IN THE NAME OF JESUS". The more I shouted that and threw fireballs, the more she crumbled. I woke up and just sat there on the edge of the bed.

Later that week, I told one of roommates the dream. He called his mom who was a pastor and told her the dream. He put her on speakerphone and this is what she said:

> "the dream wasn't a nightmare but what was to come. She said that the weight room symbolized safety and when I left the safety i.e. Weight room I was leaving my protection. The coach represented my mother watching over me, but there would come a time when I would venture out on my own with no protection it seem. The girls that were in the hallway represented trials and tribulations that I would face in life. The two girls that formed into one represented Satan;

however, because I fought back with fire and rebuked her,
I would overcome Satan. The fire represented God's word
defeating Satan.

She assured me that I would come out victorious. I asked her if she was sure about the girls in the hallway representation. You couldn't even see the lockers, and they were so many. They were on top of each other. She laughed and reconfirmed that that was what she saw.

I thanked her and left his room.

BACK IN THE DAY: PORCH TIME

Momma and I would sometimes sit on the front porch together during the spring and summer months especially if I was waiting on people to come out to play or something. We would talk about things such as the upcoming football season that I was about to have or kids in the neighborhood or girls that were interested in me or the most important one WHAT WAS SHE COOKING THAT NIGHT.

Anyway this particular day she asked me how I felt about my father? I thought that was strange because she had never ask that question before but I knew she was serious and wanted to know what my thoughts were. One thing I could say about momma and the subject of my dad was she allow me to form the opinions and views of him on my own. At that time I hadn't seen ole Keyser Soza in about three years. I told her that he was alright that I was cool with him not wanting to be involved in my life. I had her and she was all I needed.

She continued to tell me that he was in the newspaper for killing his wife. I sat there in disbelief because the last time I had saw him he was smiling with his soft spoken voice. All I kept saying was "WOW. WOW". She sat there quietly with me. I just couldn't believe it. My dad a murder. She never added or slandered him at any of the time we sat together. After about 5 more minutes of the WOW's I got myself together and ask her "so what we having for dinner? I'm thinking cube steak and rice or mash potatoes". I loved rice. She would joke and say "boy you should have been Chinese with all the rice you eat".

Even though I never got in contact with him, I thought about him occasionally wondering if he thought about me and if he knew I was alive. Sometimes a little question would run through my mind in which I would ask "why didn't he want to spend time to get to know me"? I was a good kid. Heck I played football like he did, and from the feedback from the neighborhood kids and my coaches I was pretty damn good too. I was always the first or second to go in the neighborhood or playground at school draft. So what was the problem? Besides I was getting awesome grades in school. Momma didn't play that. She would use football as my carrot to motivate me to stay out the streets and do my work in school. I remember when she sign me up for my first year of Pop Warner she told me on the way home from sign ups "if you wanna keep playing, this is the deal, no bad grades, you betta have any homework done before I get home from work. If homework ain't done then no practice or no game that week. I bet not get any phone calls from your teacher saying that you causing problems in class or school period. And finally, have that room cleaned up by the time I get home"(that one well she was lenient. Thank God because I could never seem to keep a clean room until she got sick and I took on the house chores on my own). What she was asking of me was easy. I could do that in my sleep backwards so I jumped on that deal quick, fast, and in a hurry.

Football was my first LOVE. I really didn't concentrate on nothing else while growing up. When most kids were chasing girls, I was chasing after football. If any thing or one stood in the way of me and football, I would cut them down or run through them. It didn't matter what anyone thought or said because I was in pursuit of my first LOVE and that's all I had time for.

My dad spent the next 16 years in prison. It wouldn't be until 2005 that I would talk to him again.

I Heard Somebody Was Looking
For Me...... well here I go

Hurricane Katrina had hit and we were watching it at work. The devastation, chaos, and confusion with people losing everything was surreal like watching a movie.

Some were displaced and scared that they would never get through the devastation. Some not only loss love ones they were homeless and loss everything they'd work for. One of my coworkers was from New Orleans and she was a mess because she didn't know if her family members were effected like we were watching on the news.

I had a fraternity brother and teammate who was from there as well and I was concern too. Thank God either one of us had to worry too long because we both found out everyone we were concern with was ok.

A very near and dear friend of mine had called me that evening and we got on the subject of my dad for some reason. She asked had I ever talked to him. I laughed and joked about him being too busy. He had a swamped schedule making license plates so he couldn't come to the phone at the moment.

Any way, she asked would I liked to find out where and which penitentiary he was located. In my mind I really wanted to more than anything but I played it cool and said if she could then why not. She immediately got off the phone with me and said for me to give her about 30-45 minutes and she'd call me back with what she found. For me it felt like 4-5 hours of wait time but she called way before the 30 minute deadline she had quoted me.

She told me a website to go to. We pulled it up together and she asked me if I knew his name. I laughed and told her his full name, but slyly said she probably won't find him. That was my protective mechanism to prevent me for getting my hopes up and then for them to be crushed like the other times.

I could hear her typing and then it stopped. She was quiet. She helped me navigate to the same page she was on. When I got there there he was. A photo of him. I remember her saying that's your dad alright. Ain't no denying that. Y'all look exactly alike.

I told her to shut up but thanked her. She went to another page that had an address in how to contact him. Then the big question came on the table 'Do you want to talk to him?'

I got silent and she ask why I was quiet now and she asked again did I want to talk to him?

I didn't know how to answer. I knew how I was feeling and what I truly wanted, but I was scared. What if he didn't want to talk to me. What if he didn't know who I was or just he knew who I was but didn't want to write back.

She knew with my silence I was bothered so she asked what was on my mind, what was I thinking. Anytime I started acting all serious and not joking she knew something was wrong so I told her what I was thinking.

She went on and did one better to lighten the conversation. She said she knew he'd write back if nothing else but to send one of those prison pose pictures of him against a wall out in the yard, he'll write you back don't worry she said. Then she asked if he knew momma had passed. I told her he probably didn't even know MC Hammer wasn't rapping anymore and that Hammer had went bankrupt tried to resurrect his career to flop again. We laughed and then she recommended I write him. She said he would love to hear from me. It might surprise him. I would be the last person he'd expect to receive a letter from. "You blockhead". She always called me that as her inside joke.

So that night I wrote him. I started off by saying that I didn't really see him nor saw him as a bad person for not being in my life. I continued on to say that I really didn't care about the past what was done was done and in the past what we needed to concentrate on and what we had was now. I also said that momma never spoke negative about him in my presence. She wouldn't allow it. I later in the letter told him she had passed in 1997 but I continued to finish school and went on to receive a master's degree. I explained how I had lived in Illinois for two and half years before moving back to North Carolina. I told him that I followed in his footsteps with playing football and had not only played in high school but went on and played in college in which I was awarded Academic All American honors. I went on in the letter to apologize by not pledging the fraternity he had pledge but was a part of starting another one that was a part of the Divine 9 group of historical black fraternity and sorority. I ended the letter by saying I loved him and hope to hear from him and for him to stay safe and to keep his head up. I signed it His Son, Asim Suah Khalfani.

About two weeks later, I received a letter from him in the mail. Here I was at 27 acting like I did when I met him when I was 6 some 21 years ago. I tore open the letter and read it. It was like me getting mail back from one of my favorite women movie star crushes like Pam Grier, Rosie Perez, or Janet Jackson or somebody. I probably read that letter about two or three times that day. I couldn't believe he wrote me back.

Santa Clause is real and I have proof.

I called my friend and thank her about four or five times for finding him and encouraging me to write him. She wanted to know how he was doing and when he was getting out. I told her that I didn't know that information because we hadn't discuss it in our initial letter. She asked would I write him again. I joked and said she was pushing the envelope and I didn't know. Once again, she encouraged me to write him again based off the initial response from this letter. Again I felt afraid and nervous what if he was just being nice because no one else was writing him. Again I didn't want to be disappointed with having my hopes crushed. I expressed it to her and she reassured that if he was thinking that I wouldn't had been holding the first letter in my hand from him. Besides with how I expressed not making him feel guilty for not being there gave him peace so I needed to stop thinking negatively. Blockhead!

I decided later that night to give it a try again but this time I included my cell phone number and said if he ever needed someone to talk to then call. It didn't matter what time or day just call when he was free. Now I knew he had all the free time in the world. What else could he be doing besides reading, eating, sleeping, or working out doing pushups?

HELLO.... IS IT ME YOU'RE LOOKING FOR

One day when I got off work my cell phone rang. Low and behold the voice stopped me dead in my tracks. I couldn't believe my ears on the other end of the phone.

IT WAS MY DAD-Keyser.

He asked did he catch me at a good time. "Hell yeah" in my Stone Cold Steve Austin voice on Monday Night Raw. I wasn't doing nothing but sitting here watching *The Grinch.*" *That's a line from the movie Next Friday.*

We had an awesome conversation over the phone during which I asked when he was getting out of prison. He said it would be soon; that they were planning to allow him to go home during some weekends in some months. I thought that was great. I expressed I was proud and happy for him. He ask me was I married and did I have any children? My response like I always tell people I'm the last of the Mohicans. I'm as single as a one dollar bill. And no I don't have any "packages" running around here that I knew of.

If there were some, then the baby momma needed to give me that social security number so I could claim them on my taxes!

We laughed, and he advised me to take my time finding the right one. The right one would appear when I least expected it. Then his tone changed he said that if he had had someone share that advice with him, but I stopped him. I reassured him that sometimes the road we travel is one we never knew about and all we can do is learn from it and move on. Besides he was about to be a free man.

Like I said earlier, I don't do darkness if I can help it. Just laughter and light spirits. Like Evilene, the bad witch, sung in The Wiz's *"Don't Nobody Bring Me No Bad News".*

He said he had to go but he would talk to me soon. I talked to him about five or six more times over the phone but I never saw him even after he was released from prison.

I Don't Wanna Play Anymore-Die Hard 3: The Third Attempt on My Life

I was 30 years old. You would have thought that I would have been satisfied with the accomplishments that I had achieved. Graduated from high school, college, graduate school inspite of the most trying times in my life. I was now working for myself for little under two years. I had attempted to start a non profit for underprivileged at risk youth. I had a 2004 black Beamer 325i fully loaded. I stayed by myself made good money and had clientele, was a youth mentor at the church I attended. I even had been featured two more times in two separate newspapers, BUT I still felt empty and I still hated myself. Though women adored me and gave me company and spent time with me, I still hated myself and wanted more.

At that time I thought I should be the owner of a BMW 750Li and had a townhouse or condo. I should have, I thought, been further than where I was. I mean look at people my age at 30 in investment magazines and featured in health magazines. I had recently lost all my money to some poor advice given to me by an investor who I later found out was just starting out in the field and in his career.

> Oh well Job said it best ""*Naked I came from my mother's womb, and naked I will depart. The Lord gave and the Lord has taken away; may the name of the Lord be praised.*""
>
> Job 1:21 NIV

The girl I was dating at the time lived in another state so it was my first ever long distance relationship. She would fly down or I would fly up for us to see each other. She was my Rosie Perez. At the time, I had a thing for Latinas. It was something about their spicy, fiery attitude. I could remember Rosie Perez dancing at the beginning of *Do The Right Thang* I would play that part over and over. Momma would come in the living room and fuss at me because I wouldn't play the whole tape just that part. She said I could pop the tape that way just playing one part of the video. The way that they spoke that Spanish and English together sometimes in the same sentence drove me muy loco.

Anyway back to our regularly scheduled program show. We spent Christmas together and on my way back we were talking over the phone. She didn't want to be in a long distance relationship any longer and wanted to break it off because she felt we were wasting each other's time not being able to see each other more. So within about a two week period it was over.

Also a contract I was working on closing fell through that I thought I was ready to take on.

All of these things kept piling up one after the other-losing all my investments, losing my woman, and losing the corporate deal. I was just done.

One night I thought I had had enough. I took some painkillers and chased it with bottles of Absolut Voka AND Seagrams Gin.

I was done I thought. All I kept saying was "I don't wanna play anymore". The more I recited that I didn't wanna play anymore, the more I drank and popped pills.

I passed out on my bed. I was awaken by an urge to vomit. When I staggered to the bathroom I made it just in time. What I vomited I had never seen come out of any human being. It was grayish black and I couldn't stop it from coming out. It filled the whole toilet bowl to the point that that's all I saw.

When I finished I sat on the edge of the bed and was angry at God. Here I am wanting to throw in the towel and He still wanted me in the game.

I finally laid back down and dozed off to sleep. The next morning I called my friend who had help me with finding my dad in prison and told her what I attempted to do. She listened and then said "it wasn't your time to go yet. Asim with all you've accomplished in 30 years He ain't done with you yet". She said she was getting on a bus and for me to pick her up at the bus station that night. I did. She stayed with me for 5 days. I really am grateful and thankful for her being there in such a dark time in my life. We talked, laughed, and she encouraged. She kept pointing out with all my mother had sacrificed during the time she was on this earth, for me to attempt suicide and then fail it wasn't like me. Heck everything that I tried I accomplished so it wasn't my time to go yet. God had more for me to do. "You blockhead". She made me promised before she got on the bus to go to promise her I would never do something that stupid again.

I promised her and thanked her. I thank her again she knows who she is out there.

THANK YOU. THIS CHAPTER IS FOR YOU.

FROM GHETTO TO GLORY:
THE REAL LIFE STORY OF JOB

PART 2

Pursuit of Happyness

Job experience #2

It was the end of the the summer of 2011. I was trying to keep it together with keeping my doors opened in business. At that time I had been in business for myself for 4 years. I was blessed to still have an apartment in which I was the sole occupant, a 2004 BMW 325i, other things. I never was delinquent on any bill. I paid everything when it was due.

Pursuit of Happyness was out on DVD and I would watch it at least once or twice on a weekly basis. Every time I finished watching it l would ask myself what would I do if I were in a similar situation?

Would or could I get through a situation like what I had watched?

Would or could I handle adversity the way Will Smith did?

Little did I know things were about to change drastically in which I would see if I could or not soon.

I was invited to go to the beach with a friend in which I needed to escape from the hustle and bustle that was going on in my life at the time. That was the second time I had been to the beach in my lifetime. The first time was when I was 8 years old, and my older sister and I had the opportunity to fly up to Newark, New Jersey to visit my aunt for the summer. During the time up in Jersey, we all went to the beach. I wouldn't return to the sandy beaches until 32 years later.

I enjoyed myself thoroughly. My mission was to leave every care, every problem, everything back in Charlotte, North Carolina and I did.

When I returned, my problems still were there waiting like nagging kids. So I picked up where I had left off before leaving for the beach.

I started to get behind on bills. First it was my cellphone in which I would have to pay the month plus a late charge. Then came the electric bill. I let that one get three months in the hole. Then came the rent. Then the car note. I was getting over my head and things didn't look like it was easing up any time soon.

I started to adopt the mentality of robbing Peter to pay Paul each month. Some companies were getting short changed at the end of the month because I just didn't have it. Then it happened. I got so over my head that I faced having to move out of my apartment. My cellphone had been cut off for at least two months by then. The electricity had been cut off for a month. Some nights I would be in the dark. I would use the natural light as my light to move around during the day. I started staying more nights over my girlfriend's apartment not solely for the fact that I missed her but because I didn't have heat or running water. I would bring over my clothes and ask if it was ok and if she minded if I did laundry over there.

She said she didn't and heck some nights she would even cook for her, her son, and myself.

She was a fabulous cook. The type of cook that was old school like those southern, down home, soul food cooks that'll slap the taste out your mouth type of cooks.

Anyway it had got so bad that I just started staying over there instead of my place. Then one night we were talking and she suggested that I move in. In my head I was all for it but my mind wasn't. She suggested that I get a storage unit and put my things in there and just take my clothes and move them over at her place. She said she didn't mind.

Then the imaginable happened. One morning I went out from her apartment and the car had been repossessed. I was so hurt. I broke down and started crying right in front of her.

Heck I didn't care. My whole world had been taken from me month after month it seemed.

No phone,
Then no apartment.
No food sometimes.

Now no car. It would be a few months in which I landed a job on the opposite side of town. For me to get over there would be a true challenge with no real transportation, but that's not the "Our way". You do what needs to get done no matter what.

This was my new travel schedule to get to work by 8:30a. I would get up at 6a ride my dirt bike to the bus stop because my girlfriend stay off a bypass that didn't have bus stops. So because of that I would ride to the bus stop on a bike. Then once I got to the stop, catch a bus to take me to the main bus hub/station, catch a train that would take me to another semi bus hub where I would catch another bus. I would ride that bus to a bus stop near my job, get off and ride my bike. All that travel would last about two hours and 15 minutes.

How do I know exactly how long it took?

Because that left me 15 minutes to shower before seeing my first client for the day. I would work twelve hours and then get off exactly at 830pm. No more or less because I had to be on the 845p bus because that was the last bus that came out to my job. Ride that bus to catch the train to take me back downtown. Once getting downtown I would catch the bus towards my girlfriend's apartment. The only difference was the bus wouldn't go as far down to my original bus stop that I caught the bus in the morning. Because of that I had to ride my bike for about 10-15 minutes before arriving to her apartment. I wouldn't get in until around 11:30p depending on if there were a lot of people on the bus before I got to my stop. Once getting to the apartment I still have to prepare my work plans for the next day and take a shower. So I wouldn't actually go to bed until after midnight. This was my schedule from Monday through Saturday. Sunday for me was truly a rest day literally.

This went on for 4 months until I moved in with a roommate that was close to my job.

Even though I was blessed to stay with my girlfriend, I was without a permanent place to call my own for 9 months. While staying with her I lived out of a laundry basket because all my things were in boxes in storage and I was force to be a food stamps.

During that time no one ever suspected what was going on or what I was going through during the 9 month period.

I never missed a day of work and majority of the twelve hours I was working I took only one or two breaks during the entire shift. I would take power naps sometimes in the locker room before having to go back and work with my clients.

I thank all the individuals who were supportive, friends and family, old and new, if all you did during the time was give me a kind word or words of encouragement or an ear to just listen, thank you. Sometimes that was all I needed. Whatever was given all of it I appreciate from the bottom of my heart.

Again, thank you Jehovah Jireh (the God who Provides) for keeping me through it all and showing me not to put my faith in a broken cisterns. My focus should always be put in the living water and unbreakable cistern, you, God Almighty. He is faithful even if we aren't sometimes. Thank you for your goodness, mercy, and grace.

Jesus Take The Wheel: Die Hard 4-the Fourth attempt on my life

I had been working at my job for about 9 months saving for a car.

Nothing spectacular just something to get me around town. I saw on Craigslist a 1997 Honda Accord that I liked. It was in decent condition and it ran really well.

The most important aspects was it was good on gas and maintenance/upkeep on the car was great. I didn't want to purchase something that I was constantly putting money in the gas tank or putting money in the upkeep. I learned that lesson when I had the BMW.

Yes I loved the car BUT the upkeep and gas prices were a beast. It took premium gas and an oil change was over a hundred bucks. Heck to change a headlight bulb was thirty-five to forty-five dollars. I remember I had to get brake work done eight hundred dollars for brakes, rotors, and the tires adjusted.

Now don't get me wrong the perks were amazing. Steering wheel radio control, leather seats, thermostat to tell you the temperature outside, automatic seat adjustment and I can go on and on. I love my Beamer. Just the sound when you cranked it up.

MY WORD! Makes my heart flutter.

It's expensive to ride in style.

So I had experienced the high life I was ok with keeping it simple.

One night I had visited a friend and caught a flat. I called AAA to come and help me change my tire. They did and I went on about my night. That next morning I drove to work because I had planned to go and get another tire to replace the one that had the flat that previous night.

When I got off a work, I noticed the car was making this strange sound. At first, I thought it was the radio, but when I turned the radio down, the sound wasn't noticeable so I kept on going. I got on the highway and headed to the tire shop. I got in the middle lane and that strange sound came back again. This time it was louder. I turned the radio completely off to investigate what in the heck was that sound coming from.

I got on the next highway that would take me to the tire shop. About three miles into traveling down the highway, the driver side tire fell completely off the car.

The weight of the car fell on the tire so it couldn't go anywhere. Cars swerved to other lanes to prevent hitting me. I got out of the car. Then the most horrific thing that I could imagine happened. A 18-wheeler Mack truck came up on me. All I could hear was the driver blowing its horn as it approached me and the car. I froze in fear and threw my hands in front of my face to prevent being hit.

Pause.

I use to look at movies where before the guy or girl got hit, they would throw their hands in front of their face. I would criticize and laugh and ask what were they doing?

Now I know the answer. It's an involuntary response. Thank God the Mack truck swerved and hit a car's side view mirror as they both attempted to prevent causing an accident. I ran off to the side of the highway nervous as hell to call 911 for a cop to come and direct traffic. As I was waiting I prayed in every language possible that no one would get hurt. The police came and got behind my car with their lights on to get cars to slow down as they approached the scene. When they took me to my car they were very cautious but could see I was a nervous wreck. As we got up to the vehicle they saw that lug nuts had come completely off the wheel and the only thing that was keeping the wheel on the vehicle was the weight of the car. The two officers had never seen anything like that before in their life.

They said I was lucky that no motorists were injured or myself. One cop said about two weeks before that a motorist had been hit and killed because they had car problems, and had when stepping out to exit to the side of the road, was struck and killed.

I said that was nothing but God because that Mack truck was suppose to had destroyed me plain and simple.

One of the officers called a tow truck because he saw I was all nerves. When he got there, he was hooking the car up to the truck I explained what happened and he stated that the gentleman that had changed my tire the previous night had done a piss poor job with putting the spare onto the car especially seeing where the lug nuts had landed off the vehicle.

He took me to the tire shop in which I was able to get a replacement tire. I drove to my older sister's house to explain what had just happened. I still was shaking and they could see it.

My cousins were there, and one tried to lighten the mood by quoting a line from the movie **Coming To America** "Damn shame what they did to the dog". I smiled but couldn't really enjoy the line that was being used. I told everybody I needed to take nap because I wasn't any good being awake.

Another attempt. Another close call.

ABBA IS MY FATHER BECAUSE MY BIOLOGICAL DIDN'T BOTHER

I want to dedicated this song to my Abba, Father, Jehovah
'Cause he was the one who took me from a boy to a man
So as far as I'm concerned, he's my father
'Cause my biological didn't bother
Excerpts from Shaquille O'neal **Biologically Didn't Bother**

It was the end of 2012, and I was talking to my uncle about had he heard anything with regards to the whereabouts of my dad or could he find out where he was.

Later that week he called me and told me he had found information and location of where he was. My uncle has always been a good at that Perry Mason/ Ben Matlock stuff with locating people they grew up with and Keyser Sosa was one of them.

Leave it up to my uncle, ole Sharp Eye Washington, I knew he'd find something. Continue being "steady on the case, steady on the case". *(a line from the movie,* **Uptown** **Saturday Nigh**t *featuring Bill Cosby & Sydney Poitier)*

He said that he had been arrested again for domestic violence. He said go online and I could pull up the article written about the pending charge.

I thanked him and sat on the couch read the newspaper article with my older sister and cousin. My cousin who still lived in the same city as where he was arrested suggested I should come down and pay him a visit and surprise ole Keyser maybe get some unanswered questions of why he never made efforts to stay in touch with me. My sister consigned with what she was suggesting.

A huge part of me wanted to see him and ask him why he never was a part of my life ever, what was his problem? Another part just wanted to let sleeping dogs lie.

The new year came in, and what better way than to start the new year off on a good foot. So one Sunday, I drove down to the jail to see him.

That week I had rehearsed repeatedly the conversation in my head on what he and I would talk about when I saw him.

On the ride there I was all nerves because I hadn't seen him since 1987 and now we were in 2013, 26 years later.

That was my first time ever being at the county jail in my life. I was scared as hell. What if they start pulling up things on me, pass unpaid parking tickets, stuff I stole in the cafeteria when I was in school, etc. I was like a kid waiting to go into to see the principal.

When the lady call me up, she asked if I have any electronic devices on my person and if so to say so because they had to issue me a locker key to put them inside. I was so nervous that I didn't comprehend what she was saying. Then she saw I wasn't understanding and she asked the question another way. "Do you have a cell phone"?

I was so nervous I didn't even feel my cell phone on me. I kept calling the officer "Sir" when she clearly was a "Ma'am". She could tell I was all nerves and she was very long-suffering and accommodating. I came to my senses and realized I did have a phone on me and she issued me a locker and passed me the key.

She explained how the lockers worked and how to use the key to open it; however, Simple Jack just wasn't comprehending any of her instructions. So I guess she saw this wasn't going anywhere fast and came from around her desk and walked over to the lockers with me. I felt so embarrassed. As we walked back to the desk, she asked who were I there to visit. She looked up his name on the computer then told me what floor and side he was on. She told me again the floor and side (*SIDE B*) he was on.

Good job Simple Jack.

All these Damn instructions and directions. I didn't know I was going to be taking a pop quiz to see Keyser Sosa. I felt like I was playing Nintendo's *Legend of Zelda.*

I got on the correct floor easy because I rode the elevator, but I went to the wrong end when I got off the elevator. He was located on the B side

I went to the A side. When I sat down I was just like a little kid learning how to go potty. All proud. I was just sitting there then the guard saw everyone had who they had come for but ole Simple Jack. The guard signed for me to pick up the receiver so we could talk. When I realized what he was wanting, I told him I was there to see Keyser Soza and the floor and side that the officer downstairs had said he was on.

He said you're on the wrong side.

"I BE A MONKEY'S UNCLE" as my grandma would always say.

When I got to the correct side I guess everybody that worked there had been working together and on the lookout for Simple Jack because I was Lost in Space literally.

My dad came out and sat in front of me. I was sitting there with a big Kool Aid smile. We both pick up our receivers low and behold the receivers didn't work so he motion for me to go over to the next one.

Of course we would pick a receiver that didn't work. With all the safari hunt challenges to just get to him why would the receiver just work? That would be too easy.

Once we picked up our respective receivers. I just stared at him for about four seconds. Honestly it wasn't because I was upset or anything. I was so amazed at how much we looked alike. It was like I was staring into a mirror looking at my reflection. I can honestly say he hadn't aged at all.

Mentally I was thinking "thank you for having great genes. Thank you Lawd" because he was 62 and looked like he was about 42 sitting there in front of me.

Then he said something that made my heart drop into my stomach. He asked *"WHO ARE YOU"*?

I could have jumped through the plexiglass that was separating us.

I yelled "I'm your son, Asim Suah Khalfani "! I was about to go into the genealogy of my mom and grandma and my great grandma and her mother.

Then he laughed and said I know who you are. I was just kidding with you and then he asked how I was doing and what I had been up to.

I was thinking to myself "ole Keyser Sosa got jokes. Everybody wanna be on Def Comedy Jam". I laughed at his joke and we began talking.

Now on the ride up to see him, I had a whole script that I had that I wanted to say to him; however, God had another script that He had for me to use.

Majority of the time I just listened to him about the whole reason he was back behind bars. The woman he had married was cheating on him with another man. He said actually the man would call asking for her when he was even there. He continued to say sometimes she would leave my dad at night and wouldn't return home until the next morning. She even caught a STD from sleeping around, and he had to nurse her back from it.

The night he got arrested he said he wasn't even home when the call was made by neighbors, he and his 2 year old daughter was out, and when they got home the police was waiting for him at their house. They said he had left the scene earlier and was returning.

He went on to say because he had been in prison before for murder they didn't even give him a chance to explain; they just cuffed him and locked him up.

As he explained the account of why he was back behind bars all I could do is process the fact that this man had been in the system for over half his life. Right at that moment I promised myself I would be there for my kids, my WIFE, and my family no matter what even if it killed me. This generational curse had to cease, and it was going to stop with me. Also I saw that my dad had a serious problem with choosing the wrong women. I mean with my records he was 0-2. His first marriage ended in a murder and this one caused him to be back in a place where I'm sure he didn't want to be.

We talked for about another hour then he had to go back to his cell. He said he loved me. We touched the glass and like that Keyser Sosa was gone.

To this date I haven't spoken to him again. My prayer is that he is still alive and doing well. I will never have ill feelings towards him. I love him because without him there's no me.

What I have learned from my interactions with him is some people have cameo appearances in your movie. We don't know why they have small parts but all we can do is cherish the times that they are on your SHOW.

On the way back home it was like a elephant size weight was lifted off my chest. My heart went out to him. I felt sorry and bad for him. My momma and uncle would talk about how gifted, smart, and talented he was when they were in school together, and now majority of his life had been behind bars. A real life tragedy.

Shaquille O'neal's song was made in the early '90's. He made the song as a tribute for a man, his stepfather, who stepped in and raised him from a boy to a man. I loved the song even though Shaq had no business picking up a microphone trying to rap. He was a great basketball player, but rapper, ummmmmm no Shaq-Fu.

I substituted the name that Shaquille had in the song and replaced it with the name of my Dad, my Father, my Abba. You see God has directed my path during the 37 years I've been on this earth. He has never missed a birthday, Christmas, or holiday. He's made all my football games and all my graduations.

He picked me up when I failed miserably.

He understood me when others misunderstood me.

He comforted me when no one else was available.

He loved me when I didn't see good in myself.

He loved and loves me UNCONDITIONALLY no matter how many times OR how bad I mess up.

And the great thing about Abba is He is always waiting for me to call and cry out to Him no matter what time of day.

So Abba is my Father when my biological didn't bother.

THE STOWAWAY DREAM

One night I had a dream that was both scary and disturbing at the same time. Here it is.

I was on a shipyard though I was hiding behind a wooden post that had these huge ropes winding around it, I still could see the boarding ramp leading up to the ship.

I stayed hidden because of what was about to happen frighten the heck out of me, and I didn't want any part of it.

On the deck were people, and they looked weary and tired. Their faces were dirty and dingy. Their clothes were tattered and they didn't have on any shoes on. It reminded my of serfs or slaves.

Then this hand started to put these big chains around their neck. The size of the chains reminded me of the chains that are attached to anchors on a ship that machines pull up when the ship is about to cast off. The crazy thing was the hand kept putting more chains on the people. It got so bad that the weight started pulling the people down. The people tried to stand upright; however, the hand continued to put more chains on the necks of the people. At one time I said stop putting chains on them; they can't go anywhere let alone get up. The hand didn't come over to where I was. Thank God!

I woke up and just sat straight up. I started laughing because the hand was determined to pile chains on those poor people. I remember at one time I felt lucky no one came over to where I was hiding and found me.

My aunt called me later that week, and I told her my dream because she's a very spiritual person. This is what she explained to me.

The dream meant that the people were in bondage. I was witnessing people being in some serious bondage in which they couldn't escape on their own. The hand that was placing the chains on the people was the enemy aka the devil. The enormous size of the chains represented the enormous size bondage that the people felt and were going through and because I wasn't apart of the captivity I would have something to do with freeing them. She said because they couldn't move and the chains kept weighing them down, they were looking for help and felt hopeless in their situation.

I tried to lighten the conversation by stating that the hand didn't have to keep putting chains on top of chains on those people the first chain pretty much wiped them out. I said it wasn't just men but women as well that were getting chained up. She said that was a very strong vision and asked what was I eating before I went to sleep?

We both laughed, and I said nothing in particular. She said it was something that I may be apart of that I will help people out of feeling hopeless and trapped in bondage.

She then called me Moses and Joshua out of the Bible because they helped their people out of bondage. She reminded me that God told Mae to be strong and courageous several times. She said whatever God is about to use you for that I needed to be very strong and courageous.

Before she got off the phone she reminded me again. Be very strong and courageous man of valor.

Little did I know she was warning and preparing me for what was about to transpire.

I'M NOT BUYING THAT **BRAND**
JOB EXPERIENCE **#3**

First I must say that during this last trial it brought me the closest to God than any other time in my life. As I am writing this, I'm still at awe as to how much the Lord truly loves and has kept and continues to keep me.

In undergrad I was briefly introduced to the book of Job. I read the first chapter and put the book down because I was terrified at the tests that he faced in the very first chapter. I remember I was introduced to the book by my FCA (Fellowship Christian Athletes) counselor. He recommended I read it. Little did I know one month later I would be going through my first major test similar to Job. Three tests in the first chapter?

Oh no I'll pass. Kids die... stuff stolen... health problems. Naw we good.

I told the counselor were there any "feel good" stories I could read because I just couldn't "get down" with that story. It was too hard and heavy.

It is during this final test that I've truly learned who God truly is, how much love He has for me and the characteristics of the Most High. You would think with the two previous tests and escaping near death car accidents and guns I would have been further along with my spiritual walk, but that's what makes God who he is. Gracious. Merciful. Long-suffering. Patient. There have been so many things that has been revealed during this test that sometimes brings me to my knees and just say "Thank you even in spite of me". For instance, I now truly understood the parable of the Prodigal Son and how the father waited and ran out to meet the son who left and didn't deserve forgiveness for squandering away his future that was given to him. It says that the son walking up the road (probably smelling like a pigpen and garbage) was met by his father who threw his arms around him and took his own clean robe and shoes off his feet to put around his son and on his son's feet. And then after all that, took his signet ring off and placed on his son hand and order the servants to kill one of the best, fat cattle so that they could have a feast celebration for his return.

I say all of that to show the character and love that was demonstrated from the father to the son who many would considered as a failure, but God doesn't operate under societal views. His operation is far different and much better. Before this test, I viewed the son like his brother did because I couldn't understand how the father was so forgiving and excited that the son came back and how he treated him after losing his fortune that was given to him. I remember reading this parable I use to look at the son sideways and turn my nose up at him and even put my two cents in as to what I would have done. I do know it wouldn't have been that.

One day I was watching Bishop TD Jakes and his sermon that was posted on YouTube was entitled Just Do It. He spoke about how the people of Israel knew their God which caused them to be the people that God had called them to be which in turn influenced the actions of them doing what God had called them to become confidently and boldly. Know, Be, Do!

I would learn this during my last test.

THE CHRISTMAS GIFT

On December 24, 2013, Christmas Eve I was diagnosed with multiple sclerosis. The disease to this date has effected over 400,000 people in the US and over 2 million in the world. That's just too many in my opinion. Heck just 1 person is too many in my opinion.

Multiple sclerosis is an autoimmune disease that effects the nervous system. People have lesions on their spinal cord and brain. Some can experience blurred vision, bouts of uncontrollable shaking, loss of balance, difficulty walking and standing, joint pain, brain fog, loss of memory and concentration, weak bladder, weak muscle strength, difficulty with performing fine motor skills, and etc.

On December 24, my car broke down which caused me to try to walk to a safe place to charge my phone because my battery had died to get help to assist me with the issue at hand. It was extremely cold that night and the temperature was dropping by the minute it seem so I was forced to walk to safety; however, my plans were foiled due to what was about to happen in the next couple of minutes.

Prior to that night, I didn't know what was going on with me. I knew that certain activities had started to be difficult for me to perform. On my birthday I went to the beach with my girlfriend and we were playing Putt Putt miniature golf. I had to take mini breaks during the game because it was difficult for me to get through the game. I caught myself having to use the putter to walk up the hills to the ball which was strange because I never had to use anything before for assistance to walk.

During the night my car broke down, I call my older sister to see if she could come to take me to my apartment because honestly I knew that I couldn't walk the distance that was required to get to a safe warm place. She refused because she felt that I hadn't call her in over two months so what was the need to call her now. My phone's battery life was constantly flashing warning signals that it was about to die soon so I thanked her and tried to make another call before the phone completely died.

No luck. It died due to the conversations her and I had just finished taking all the juice from the battery. So I was left without a phone and having to walk to a safe place to charge my phone so I could call someone to see if they could come help me. It was about half a mile to a mile to a local McDonald's restaurant which was the only safe place to charge the phone. My younger sister was out of town with her boyfriend and she was the only other phone number I could remember and the phone book in my phone I couldn't get to because the phone was dead. As I tried to walk to the McDonald's to charge my phone, my walking got worse and worse as I tried to walk to the McDonald's so much so that I fell several times. I had an iPad that was in a backpack that I had on. I fell so many times during my attempt that I cracked the screen of the iPad.

A police officer was driving down the street and saw I was struggling something awful and made a U-turn to come back around. As he was pulling up to the side of the sidewalk, I fell right in front of his car. He got out and immediately I yelled "I'm not drunk or under the influence of drugs" because it did look from my walking and falling that I was on something. He came up to the front of the car and asked me what was wrong. I was so weak and had fell numerous times, I couldn't even push myself up to sit up on the curb. He asked if I had anyone he could call or did I want him to call an ambulance. I answered that I had no family here in town he could reach because my only family was in Charleston which was my younger sister.

I declined for him to call an ambulance and tried to persuade him to just give me a ride to the McDonald's that was six blocks up the road. He refused and said I needed to seek medical attention so he called an ambulance. As I tried to stand up, I had no strength in my legs and would just fall completely back down. The cop told me just to relax because I just didn't have the strength to do anything. Once the ambulance came the police and I told the attendant what was going on. The attendant could clearly see something wasn't normal but I was coherent and wasn't under any influence or anything.

In the ambulance as we were traveling to the hospital, he took my vitals which were perfect. No signs of high blood pressure or irregular heartbeat. He asked what I did for a living I told him I was a personal trainer that I PRIDED myself on my health.

We continue to converse and I went on to tell him I was 235 pounds at one time and had over a 40 inch waist. I said I felt I had to be overweight because it helped me now to empathize and sympathize with my clients who struggle to lose the weight and keep it off permanently. By that time we were at the hospital.

Did I ever mention in previous chapters how I hate hospitals and how they reek of death?

Anyway we got checked in and the attendant wheeled me in the back and wished me a Merry Christmas and Happy New Year and left. When I was in the back with the nurse she asked what happened and could I explain what went on to cause me to visit them that night. I explained how my walking, balance and strength were effected which caused me to fall all over the street, but now that I had rode in the ambulance I could feel my strength and balance regaining. She put me in a wheelchair in which she asked if I could walk over to the chair or did I need assistance? Of course the 'Our way' wanted to prove I was ok so I walked over. I was a little wobbly but nothing concerning. She took my vitals and tested the strength in my legs, shoulders, and biceps. I knew what she was doing because as an athletic trainer we would do the same test if we suspected a nerve injury.

I thought that was strange. *CLUE#1*

I later was taken to an ER Room after being in the waiting room. There they took my blood and said that they wanted to do an MRI. I thought that was strange.

What did I need an MRI for? I wasn't playing football anymore or did I say anything about injuring my legs.

Oh well.

Eventually I was taking in the back to the imagining machine where they took imagines of my head. Afterwards the tech said that the doctor would be in to talk with me. I thought "what does he need to speak to me about"? *CLUE#2*

The doctor came in and tried to lighten the mood about what was going on, but I wasn't buying that brand I wanted to know what was the findings on the test. Why go to class and take an exam and the teacher never gives you the results of the performance?!

So I ask so what's the final results doc?

He went on to say the blood work, blood pressure, and all the vital test came back normal to excellent. I said that I knew it because I was in perfect health. I don't eat crazy or participate in any recreational drug activity so I knew my health would reflect that.

Then I asked about the MRI test, what did that say?

He said it was too early to say but wanted me to come back for a CAT Scan. I thought that was crazy.

Why? Why did I need to come back for a CAT Scan?

I ask "is everything ok"?

He again said they needed to see some more images.

Two weeks later I did my CAT Scan. Afterwards, I asked the attendant doing my scan what he saw when we were done. He stated he couldn't divulge that information because all he did was take the images and wasn't licenses to read and interpret what were on the images. *CLUE#3*

In my mind, that was bull. He could have told me which I knew whatever that was on those two images weren't good or favorable.

They told me to come back in two weeks to get my results. Those two weeks seem like an eternity. I got my packet of the results that were from what the two images showed. The desk clerk and I made me another appointment. She said that I needed to go to a neurologist, and he would read me what the packet of information said and the results. Of course I didn't wait that long, right when I stepped foot out of the office I opened the sealed manila envelope.

As I read, it sounded like I had multiple sclerosis. Lesions, scars, loss of strength, failure and loss of balance and coordination. I was in disbelief. What the hell was this meaning and saying. Then as I sat in the waiting room I begin to get angry at all the people who when I ask what they saw from the images they tiptoed around the request I was making.

Why the hell couldn't they just been upfront with me?

As I was driving home I called my older sister with the news that I had just found. Then I just broke down and started crying.

Why me?

What did I do to deserve this?

Hadn't I been through enough?

Why was God punishing me? Was I not one of His children?

First my grandmother succumbing to breast cancer, then my momma with Lupus, and now me, the one of the three who took PRIDE in his health and was passionate with helping others to overcome their struggle and health challenges.

This in my mind as I was thinking "this was some FUCKING BULLSHIT". How dare God turn His back or allow me to go through yet another major trial in a short amount of time. I had just within the last 2 years went through losing everything that I had worked so hard to obtain and honestly I hadn't regained any of it back. So what the fuck (WTF)!

My sister gave some advise while I was crying and driving. She said that God had this and He hadn't left nor turned away from me and that I just needed to trust Him and that He would see me through this.

At the neurologist he read and showed me the images on the screen from both the MRI and CAT Scan and ask did I exhibited or experience any symptoms prior to Christmas Eve?

Other than the summer of that year I hadn't. My walking and balance started to be effected around my birthday but other than that no.

He was amazed because based off the size of the lesions and how many of them that he was amazed that symptoms were just presenting themselves.

I asked does MS come from taking shots to the head because I played football for 11 years and took up boxing in grad school.

He explained that multiple sclerosis doesn't come from trauma to the head as an athlete who takes multiple blows repeatedly to the head. He said multiple sclerosis was from something else. He asked had I been experience loss of balance like I had of December 24th currently. I said no though I had maybe fell a couple more times before coming to see him. He suggested I may get a cane to assist with my gait but was optimistic with living with this because a lot of people continue to live fruitful lives despite having it.

In my mind I was just devastated because I just couldn't understand how in the hell did I get this? Asim has played football, basketball, softball, tennis, train for triathlons and 5k races, wrestled, boxed, took up Brazilian Ju Jitsu and Muy Thai, and took pleasure in working out and instructing others with their health again how and more importantly why?

The doctor told me of a medication to help subside the formation of new lesions and suggested I start to get on it ASAP.

I told him I don't take medicine and that I don't even take aspirin when I experience a headache or get under the weather with a common cold.

The doctor still warn me those things were less serious in comparison to multiple sclerosis. If I didn't want symptoms to get any worse than medication was the answer.

I just couldn't wrap my head around that suggestion. I was definitely not BUYING THAT BRAND. I asked him was there a cure to this because everything else that I had experience up until that point I was able to heal from. He said "No. Just treat the symptoms but no cure".

That catch phrase of "I'm not buying that brand" is something I say when faced with a situation that I don't agree with or that contradicts my beliefs. So I wasn't buying the brand that I would have to take medication for the rest of my life nor buying that I would have to live with this for the rest of my life.

The doctor made another follow up appointment with another neurologist. It was here that the journey to prove that I wasn't buying the brand of the doctors began.

A side note that needs to be addressed. How is it that the multiple sclerosis foundation has raised a ton a money on research but there hasn't been A CURE found yet? Doesn't that or shouldn't that raise questions and red flags? And this so-called research there's still no cure or strategic plan in sight? The only findings are treating the disease. There continue to be more cases of people being diagnosed. No cure though. I think that's odd. 400,000 in the US and 2 million in the world. Strange very fishy. Most of the time I say there's nothing to see here, but in this case, there's plenty to see here. A lot to investigate plenty.

So the woman I was dating at the time and I started researching what multiple sclerosis was, things that could assist with making symptoms better, and if there were any protocols, practices, procedures that were out there that we could adopt or use for me. Rocky Balboa goes back to the gym yet again to get ready for another fight.

We found different things some simple some evasive, but the goal was to find a cure.

One day I was making breakfast when my roommate asked had I ever heard of a doctor by the name of Dr. Terry Wahls?

I said "no". He suggested I look her up she had a talk on YouTube, a Tedtalk seminar. I went in the room and looked her up. She talked about her story of how she WAS diagnosed with secondary progressive multiple sclerosis and how she healed herself back to health MS free. She started out in a zero gravity chair and was bed ridden. By the time she was done within a nine (9) month period, she was walking around and back at work teaching, lecturing, and doing research. Heck she had recovered so well, she would ride her bicycle to and from work-a total of six (6) miles round trip per day.

I couldn't believe it. After watching her talk I immediately went and goggle to find out more about this doctor. I found she was releasing a book on how she did it. I quickly ordered her book on Amazon. The book would take a month before I would receive it because it wouldn't be released until the following month.

It was like waiting for Christmas. The days couldn't get here fast enough. When the book got to my house, I dove right in reading, taking notes, highlighting key points that I thought were relevant. What I found was she talked about nutrition and how eating properly and staying away from foods that had poor nutritional value was the key. One thing she suggested was to eliminate table sugar, dairy, and gluten type grains. She explained how those foods caused inflammation and the problems of MS.

Immediately I stopped eating all the categories she had suggested to eliminate. I eliminated all process foods in my diet and started to incorporate nothing but green leafy vegetables, organic meats, and healthy fats and nuts for my brain since multiple sclerosis is an autoimmune disease that attacks the brain. The switching over wasn't a hard thing for me. I knew because I really didn't eat processed food or fried foods that wouldn't be a problem as well as milk and dairy products. I was already lactose intolerant so that wasn't a problem either. The problem was the sugar but I knew I could kick it. All I could hear in my head was both my grandma and momma saying "You wanna get better, then stop eating sugar! You heard the woman". So they were motivating me internally I stopped. I can remember the exact last time I had sugar. It was Super Bowl Sunday. I was over my girlfriend's apartment watching the Super Bowl. I was eating pizza, chicken wings, and two oatmeal raisin cookies. I had a 16 oz Arizona fruit punch.

That next day I went on the Wahls protocol and never looked back.

I went back to the neurologist for the second time, though I was stronger than my first visit and stated that I had adopted a protocol from one of his colleagues in the field who had been diagnosed with multiple sclerosis, but she had cured herself and others not only from MS but also other TBIs (traumatic brain injuries).

He was concerned with what I was saying and asked me had a called the pharmaceutical company to put my order in for my medication. I asked him did he hear what I had said. He said yes but still he wanted me to make the call. Even though I had showed him documentation I was making charting my progress and any regression since starting the protocol. He still was adamant about me going on the meds regardless of what I was saying or trying to show him.

It was there that I promised myself I would never come back to his office until I was walking completely without assistance and MS free. I vowed that he would eat his words. Jehovah Rapha "the Lord will heal" would be my doctor not a "white coat".

GOD DOESN'T WATER A WELTERING OR DYING PLANT

2 Samuel 13:1-21

This story is about Tamar whose name means palm tree. She was the daughter of King David, and sister of Absalom. Her mother was Maacah, daughter of Talmai, king of Geshur. According to the narrative in 2 Samuel 13, she was raped by her half-brother Amnon.

My older sister every morning during my fight back to health and cure from multiple sclerosis text me different motivational text. One morning this is the text I received:

GM.... What are you holding onto that you need to let go of? II Samuel 13:1-21 Tamar means palm tree... A palm tree never dies and whatever has happened in your life God has brought you through it and you are a Survivor!! It is time to STAND on God's word TODAY and know he LOVES YOU and will see you through all your trials Child of God! BE ENCOURAGED!!!!!!

That night I was having a ledge-type of moment where I was feeling rejected and defeated with trying to stay positive and optimistic with dealing with the MS and feeling sorry for myself with all the trials I had overcome. I was just mentally drained and spiritually tired.

One of my middle school friends and ex girlfriend had called me per my request to cheer me up.

I told her how I was feeling and what I was thinking with all the things that I had already experienced-

1. The death of my grandmother
2. The sickness of my mother

3. *The death of my mother*
4. *The lost of my possessions and money*
5. *The numerous car accidents*
6. *The being shot at, guns pulled out on me*
7. *The failed suicide attempt*
8. *The absence of my father even though I felt I was a good kid and how I had to raise myself from a boy to a man*
9. *And now the fight for my health with MS*

I just couldn't see me fighting anymore and much longer. How much more could a person take?

She listened and allowed me to vent.

Afterwards, she gave me her advice. I thank her because it was so powerful. So much so I needed to put it this book and give it a chapter. My hopes is it blesses these words of encouragement from both women of God can encourage and shine hope in someone else journey that's reading this chapter like it blessed and touched me.

Thank you Princess Asthma.

She started by saying that God has a major calling on my life. With all the things that I had experienced that I would be painfully mistaken to believe that He had brought me this far to just leave me especially now that I looked to Him for EVERYTHING.

She continued with God doesn't water a weltering or dying plant. He takes care of those that have purpose and destined to be used in His kingdom. With what I had been through, most people that we grew up with didn't make it this far. Some are no longer with us. She suggested I was destined for greatness-great things were in the horizon I just had to hold on a little while longer.

She continued and likened my experiences to a gardener pruning, cutting, and shaping his rose bush to be on display for those to enjoy. She asked me did I think that a person would put their resources into an investment if they knew that there wouldn't be a return on the investment?

I answered "No".

She continued on with her point by asking then why would God invest all that time with keeping me and sheltering/shielding me if He wasn't going to carry me through this test?

She continued by repeating something that I said to her in a previous conversation that her and I had, if I compared my trials to Job's then I knew what was the outcome to Job going through the tests-he got double for his trouble. She suggested and recommended that I just hold on and stay faithful and focus as Job did because God hadn't brought me this far to leave me. She said the devil has NO POWER over me because he was defeated at the cross when Jesus died. He's powerless and he knows it. The only weapon he has is the weapon of confusion, doubt, and lies. If I listened to his cunning lies of God not wanting to heal me or He's forgotten about me, then that's the only weapon to get me to press the "pause button" a slow me down. She recommended that I stop looking in the rear view mirror and look forward keep my eyes focused on what was ahead. She went on to say God is not the author of confusion, the enemy aka the devil is.

She agreed yes I had experienced some things that maybe some hadn't but that God had a plan and purpose for me that maybe I was going through this to be able to help others during similar experiences they may be facing.

As she was saying that, immediately I thought about the dream I had had on the shipyard and my aunt and I conversation about what it meant.

I could hear my aunt's voice, "Be strong and very courageous man of valor" before she got off the phone.

Wow! I now saw where this part of the movie was taking a turn and the plot was thickening. Rocky cut his opponent and saw that he has signs of weakness too. He could win. Just hold on Rock. Hold on just a little while longer.

She finished by reminding me that God had given me visions rather it be through dreams, conversations with people or confirmations I may have heard, through things that I saw while watching tv or movies, thoughts while taking a shower, etc. It's all part of the process. We may not know what's going on when it's happening, but we have to have faith that it will turn out for the good and our benefit. God knows the ending, we don't. We just have to hold on trust and believe, and have faith while He's working out the plan.

That was the best advices that any had given me on that day. Princess Asthma saved the day. I climbed off the ledge from wanting to jump off. Then she said she was sleepy and tired and had to leave.

We both told each other good night and hung the phone up.

Don't Stop Believing

Psalm 103:3-*who forgives all your sins and heals all your diseases* **NIV**

> Isaiah 53:4-5-*Surely he took up our pain and bore our suffering, yet we considered him punished by God, stricken by him, and afflicted. But he was pierced for our transgressions, he was crushed for our iniquities; the punishment that brought us peace was on him, and by his wounds we are healed* **NIV**

These verses I have held onto through this whole process. When times I didn't see the possibility of my healing or doubt would creep in and remind me of my current situation and me not receiving my healing yet. These two verse along with Jeremiah 37:27 which says *I am the Lord, the God of all mankind. Is anything too hard for me? NIV*

I would even go to Hebrews 6:18 where it talks about it being IMPOSSIBLE for God to lie.

> *God did this so that, by two unchangeable things in which it is impossible for God to lie, we who have fled to take hold of the hope set before us may be greatly encouraged NIV.*

I eventually went back to read the book of Job because I had to know what was the final outcome of his horrific tests in his life. It was there that I learned that when his health failed him along with his friends providing negative advise and be counterproductive, that Job kinda allow some doubt and negativity to creep in. Even though he was pleading his case to his friends that he had done no wrong in the eyesight of God, they still didn't believe him. I found that I too though none of my closest friends were throwing that type of salt on my wound, I myself was the worst enemy that I was battling.

It was at times, I wished I had never been born, that one of the car wrecks that I had experienced wasn't so generous as to allow me to walk away. I even thought about how blessed I was to have survived the numerous gun incidents and why God had sparred me. How He carried and covered me to leave me in the desert to die of thirst and hunger.

I started to really doubt this whole journey based on one winter night.

I had to walk home because my car wouldn't start. It wasn't a far walk just about four to six apartment units up from where the car was parked. I got out the car I was doing fine for the first couple of units. It was the final apartment units that was given me problems with my walking. By the time I approached the last unit that was where my apartment was located the symptoms that I had experienced on Christmas Eve came back. I tried to walk over to where some cars were parked to just hold or lean on until I got myself together.

I fell right near the back bumper of one of the parked cars. I hurried to get in between them just in case someone came out and saw me. I leaned on one of the parked cars for a little while while I tried to regain my composure and strength. I kept saying to myself "you only got *100 yards* left come on Lamail get it together".

The pep talk was to no avail because I didn't have it in me. So the only thing left was to crawl. I started crawling in the parking lot towards my apartment door. I was so focused I didn't see a guy coming out to throw his garbage in the dumpster. When he saw that I was struggling to get to the door, he dropped his trash along with another gentleman who was making a flower delivery. He saw the same thing. He got out his van because by that time I was directly in the parking lot and cars coming down and coming up couldn't travel due to me being in the middle. They both came to my rescue.

I was so freaking embarrassed. They asked was I ok. I told them a lie. I stated that I had twisted my knee getting out of the car and couldn't put pressure on my leg. So the trash guy told the delivery guy had would help me to the apartment because I told them both if I could get to the door I would be fine. He helped me to the door. I thanked him and stood by the door until he left. When I opened the door I immediately fell to the floor again. Luckily no one was home. I crawled to my room and onto the bed. Once I relaxed for about 10 minutes everything came back strength and all.

About two weeks had passed and one of my collegiate friends called to check up on how I was doing. I told her that I was doing fine. I informed her that I had made a decision after this last doctor visit to the neurologist my next visit would be my final visit because they just wanted to put on meds not to cure what was going on but to treat symptoms not cure.

Because she's in the medical field she strongly suggested that I continue to go to the neurologists and that I make the call to start taking the drugs.

I made an analogy. If a person has a massive oil leak requiring them to take their car in to be service. When taking the car in, the mechanics take the car in the back for service. When they come back out, they say "you had a massive oil leak so what we did was put some duck tape on to stop the leak from spilling on the streets as you drive".

The problem is still there. They haven't addressed anything. I told her that's what I was feeling. He wasn't addressing the problem just putting duck tape on the symptoms. No cure just treatment.

I continued by asking her a question "why would God design a body to get sick and not have a cure to fix it"? I continued by quoting Psalms 103:3 that God made a promise in His word that stated He would heal me of ALL my diseases. Not some but ALL. I continued to say how is it he takes and heals you when you get a common chest cold, but he can't cure this?

What kinda God is that?

I don't wanna follow or serve that type of GOD.

Why call Him Jehovah Rapha "the Lord who heals" and now one of your children is sick, and he's looking to you and you are nowhere to be found?

I ended my closing argument by saying that 60% of Jesus' ministry while He was on the earth during His last three years dealt with healing the sick. Jesus went to the cross and bore my illness. I asked her had she ever seen the movie, *The Passion*, because the beating he took and the nails that nailed Him to the cross was my disease that was nailed up there with him that day He died.

We both got quiet, and she suggested if I was that adamant, then I shouldn't go after this next visit.

I went to the appointment and saw the neurologist. At the visit, I had improved again since I had seen the first neurologist.

We talked and again I told how I was following a protocol of a doctor who had been diagnosed with secondary progressive MS and how she returned back to optimal health. I told of her story and even gave where she could be found on YouTube and her book. I explained that nutrition was the key.

Though she was interested she still suggested I go on medication. She looked at my chart and saw I was recommended to be on one particular medication. She exclaimed that was strange because the medication that the first "white coat" wanted to put me on would not work well with my ethnicity. I looked at her and shook my head. She went on to say she wanted me to try two other brands of medication for MS, but we needed to do blood work to determine which was the best one. She continued before she left to say medication A had a slim chance of giving me a brain tumor and medication B had a slim chance of giving me a heart tumor. I couldn't believe what she was saying. Medicine 1 that was recommended didn't work well with Blacks. Med A could cause a brain tumor, and Med B could cause a heart tumor.

Another footnote, you ever notice how on those Med commercials the people look so happy until at the end the guy rambles off in the background all these side effects. I thought this pill was going to help me keep an erection not cause death. I just wanted to have sex with my wife not for her to cash in on my life insurance policy and become a widow.

So sad to say that proved as she was stating her spill about med A and B it reiterated I definitely will not be buying this brand nor any brand other than healing and curing me. I also made it up in my mind that if God wouldn't heal me naturally that I was willing to die but I wouldn't take medication.

I continued to try Dr. Wahls program however I wasn't getting the same results which was disheartening. I still held on to God's word because He said He couldn't lie, and all the other times He showed up and showed out. It wasn't until one day I was in my room praying when my roommate came in and asked had I ever heard of a doctor by the name of Dr. Sebi? He continued to explain that Dr. Sebi was the only doctor who and ever cured AIDS and other "incurable" diseases. He gave me the YouTube video to look him up. Once he left my room, I looked him up.

In 1987, he was arrested and brought in front of the Supreme Court based on his claims of curing AIDS. He won but more importantly he was a person who was facing poor health before he became an herbalist. As a 30 year old man, he was experiencing bad cases of asthma, high blood pressure, impotency and erectile dysfunction. He had worked with famous people like Steven Segal, Lisa "Left Eye" Lopez, Michael Jackson, and many more. He was the doctor who helped cure Ervin 'Magic' Johnson of his AIDS. The man is amazing that was the answer I was searching for. Ask, seek, knock.

Dr. Sebi the herbalist. He has cured every disease known to man based on nutrition and herbs.

He believes that every disease starts out the same and if you address the root cause you put the body back into its rightful place and order to heal itself.

He went a step further than Dr. Wahls by saying how we are eating a lot of hybrid types of food thinking we are eating foods that are organic.

Our bodies work from minerals such as carbon and cooper for the brain, calcium for the bones, iron for the blood, etc. Our bodies need 102 essential minerals though because of our poor choice of nutrition we are depriving ourselves which cause problems. It made sense. He went on to explain that every disease starts from the break down of the mucus membrane. The mucus membranes main job is to protect us from foreign invaders that we come in contact with rather it be intentionally like wearing colognes, scented lotions, or perfumes or unintentionally. Once the mucus membrane is comprised, the stuff spills into the blood being absorbed in the body. He also spoke on the importance of fasting. Fasting has been around since the Old Testament times. When you fast, the body has a greater chance to heal itself because it isn't obstructed with having to digest food.

Any way I followed his suggestions. ALL OF THEM even giving up meat altogether and becoming a vegetarian.

THE MIRACLE HEALING

Jesus looked at them and said, "With man this is impossible, but with God all things are possible."
mat.19.26.niv

When I first was diagnosed with multiple sclerosis I was really bad off in my opinion.

For one my sleeping position changed drastically. I couldn't sleep but in one position and that was on my back with my right leg bent and my left being straight. NO EXCEPTIONS.

This was because I had tried other positions but all would cause me severe cramping to the point of not when I would get out of bed bed to walk around in my room, sometimes I would have to crawl to the bathroom to do number one or number two because my legs would be dead or poor circulation towards them. Even if I hadn't been sleeping, I would have to lean forward on the wall to urinate when I went to use it.

I had to put my hands on beside my sides because they would tingle and go to sleep. Sometimes the would fall asleep so much that I feared that if I fell on them or rolled on them, I couldn't differentiate rather I had broke them from the fall or whatever the case my have been during the period that I was experiencing it. My right pinky was starting to involuntarily stay balled.

At the time that, I tingling and stiffness was felt in my feet as well and it was hard to flex them when I sat on the side of the bed.

It was times that taking a shower and shaving my face were a challenge because my hands would shake violently. I had to sit on the toilet to dry myself from taking showers because my balance wasn't good to stand and perform the task. I can't count how many times I dropped and broke dishes due to my grip becoming weaker than before being diagnosed.

My handwriting began to be effected in which I couldn't sign my name nor just write a simple Thank you note. My typing on the computer also was a challenge because I started to have to pecking at the keyboard instead of fluently using the home row keys and moving easy and effortlessly.

My bladder had become so weak that if I didn't immediately relieve myself I would have an accident sometimes having to take showers and change everything that I had on.

Falling was beginning to be a normal thing so I was use to the wobbling that took place and me missing steps that would throw my balance off causing me to fall to the ground.

Grocery shopping was a huge event and chore. I couldn't go to the grocery store for an extended period of time with me being drained energy wise, and I would use the grocery carts to be a walker to maneuver around the grocery store. I had to start using a walking cane which I never really got comfortable with walking with not because I was embarrassed but because I didn't use it while I was in my apartment. When coming home it wasn't anything for me to make about six to eight trips when in the past it probably only took two or three. I couldn't take too many bags at a particular time because it effected my balance. Sometimes I needed assistance with bringing the bags in or would have individuals just bring the groceries in altogether.

I felt that I had become an infant at the age of 35-36. I had went backwards where it seemed to me most adults were striving in their lives.

But like Job i kept holding on to His word. He said it was IMPOSSIBLE for Him to lie and by the beating that Jesus took at the cross, I am healed.

> *Surely he took up our pain and bore our suffering, yet we considered him punished by God, stricken by him, and afflicted. But he was pierced for our transgressions, he was crushed for our iniquities; the punishment that brought us peace was on him, and by his wounds we are healed."*
>
> Isaiah 53:4-5 NIV

I went on YouTube everyday and watched Dr. Sebi for encouragement and guidance as well as individuals who had received healing through the instructions he provided on how to go about the healing process.

I went on a 40+ day fast only consuming water, homemade juice, and the herbs Dr. Sebi and his counsellors recommended. I was determined to get back to glory no mattered what anyone- friend, foe, "white coat", anyone had to say.

One week it started happening, the symptoms started to progressively get better.

First I noticed the strength in my bladders in which I could hold my bathroom breaks longer and longer without having to rush to get to the toilet. Then I noticed that I was leaning against the wall and could stand up straighter and straighter. The symptoms began to get better and better and lesser and lesser.

One day I noticed I could not only lie in both sides, but could lie on my stomach like I use before being diagnosed.

The last couple were the final HALLELUJAH moment. The tingling in both hands began to lessen daily and then it happened. My balance started to get better and better. I wasn't all over the place when I stood and I didn't have to hold on to furniture to walk down the hallway to my room.

And then my walking started to correct itself in which I not only had to use a cane but I was walking normally like I had been before the MS started. I was able to run. I hadn't run let alone jogged in over two years.

During this whole journey with multiple sclerosis it taught me how I to appreciate the small things that get overlooked on a daily basis.

I now have a new appreciation for every chore and task I have to perform daily and take pleasure no matter how long or short the duration to complete it. Always count your blessings and the people that are in your life.

> *I leave with this. It was also one of the verses I mediated on many a days.*
>
> *Jesus replied, "Truly I tell you, if you have faith and do not doubt, not only can you do what was done to the fig*

tree, but also you can say to this mountain, 'Go, throw yourself into the sea,' and it will be done. If you believe, you will receive whatever you ask for in prayer."

mat.21.21-22.niv

His Eyes Are On the Sparrow/ His Eyes Were Watching God

"I love the Lord, for he heard my voice; he heard my cry for mercy. Because he turned his ear to me, I will call on him as long as I live."

Psalm 116:1-2 NIV

I never lose hope but my faith was tested in the trials I faced.

Was I scared?

Hell yes!

There were times I questioned God as Job did but what kept me standing firm and not moving was His word and His promises. You see God doesn't operate like us mortals, and thank Goodness He doesn't because....

Every night before bed after praying, I would remind Him of His promises and more importantly, I would remind myself.

When I was in high school and there were unanswered questions, uncertainty on the outcome of my mother hanging in the wings, I would ask and ponder will I have to migrate to the street life to becoming a professional drug dealer even though I didn't want to and had stayed away from that life when some of my friends were running to the fast money, cars, and girls/popularity. I prayed and begged that He wouldn't take my mother from me because I wasn't ready and I didn't know what I would do if she left so soon. So for those four years, I mentally prepared for her dying and not being around much longer.

After her death, I remembered telling some of my friends when they would ask "how did you do it"?

My first response was "God." Then I would continue by saying "I was on borrowed time with her after my sophomore year of high school", but I knew that I had to look to Him for my sanity and strength.

Then when I lost everything-investments, money, clients, cell phone, apartment, car, I again even though it was difficult getting up two hours before work and getting home sometimes four hours after work, I use to listen to gospel songs on my Blackberry phone that kept me, encouraged me, motivated me to continue to look to Jesus who was the author and finisher. The Alpha and Omega, beginning and end. So even though I sometimes complained and couldn't understand what was going on. I knew He said that He would never leave nor forsake me.

Then this last trial/test I just couldn't understand.

Why?

Why me Lord? What did I do that was so wrong in your eyesight that would cause yet another devastating blow to me?

Yes, I cursed God even say that I wanted alliance with the devil because I felt that God didn't love me nor care about me, but deep down in my spirit I knew was a lie, and I didn't want to leave His presence so I kept on praying and believing. I remembered telling a close friend "I'm putting it all on black. I'm putting ALL my chips on black. I'm going ALL in". All I knew was that He had kept me with the last two major tests, and car wrecks, and gun incidents where I didn't get hurt or killed, He had to come through with this one it had to fit the model and format of the rest of my life.

The lady with the blood issue, who had went to all the medical professionals in the land to sought out advice with her issue; she had exhausted her funds but found no solution, but she had heard of a man who was healing the sick, giving sight to the blind, bringing back the dead. She thought if I can touch the hem (not arm, not leg, not hand, not foot, not head or back) but the hem of His garment she would receive her healing, and she did.

God is so faithful even when we aren't to Him. There is NO challenge big or small that He can't fix.

Thank God for my brother, Jesus, who died not only for my sins, but the reconciliation back to His Father, my dad.

And the great thing is I don't or never did deserve it but He loved me so.

In all my test and trials I can honestly say He not only showed up but He showed up AND showed out.

I will always have my eyes fixed on the sparrow. I will always be watching God until the day I return home to meet Him.

> **"I love the Lord, for he heard my voice; he heard my cry for mercy. Because he turned his ear to me, I will call on him as long as I live."**
>
> Psalm 116:1-2 NIV

Can I Get An Encore?

These are 7 other books that I am planning to write that stem from the things I have read and researched while going through my last trial of life with multiple sclerosis. During the time of researching, reading, and watching videos to get my health back, it showed me that some of my family members died prematurely i.e. my grandmother, grandfather, whom died way before I was born during the time my mother was still a child, and my mother could have lived longer than they did. The foods that they ate, lifestyles they were living, and the foods that they knew nothing about could have increased their years on this earth with their love ones.

My grandfather I never got a chance to meet so I don't know how long he was on this earth. My grandmother died when she was 63-64. My mother passed at the young age of 44.

The 7 book series is geared towards topics on nutrition, health, fitness and daily motivation. The books foundations are taken from the Bible and dedicated to the people who I loved dearly, Yvette, Mae and Charlie, who I never met.

1. The White Coats: the myths, mirages, and illusions of the medicine industry (Revelation 22:2). This book exposes the lies and underlying agenda of the medicine world and how it's a billion dollar a year industry whose goal is to keep us sick with no answer or resolution in sight.

2. How The Devil Snuck In Through The Back Door: The Flimflam Of Food

   (Genesis 1:29). This book discusses how certain everyday foods we eat are laced with harmful chemicals that have the same neurotransmitters as addictive hardcore drugs such as codeine, heroine, and cocaine as well as foods that cause hormonal changes in our body.

3. Strange Bedfellows: The Rat Race Against Time

   (Ezekiel 47:22). This book looks at how the FDA gets the masses sick and the pharmaceutical companies keep the masses sick with **treating** our illnesses instead of **curing** them.

4. Benjamin Button and the Fountain of Youth: How to reverse the aging process

   (Book of Daniel-chapter 1). This book lies down the root cause of disease and a nutritional eating regiment that is based on foods that heal and reverse the disease process to get and keep the body healthy.

5. Halftime adjustments: embracing mistakes to succeed (Proverbs 3:5-6). A book about embracing mistakes and learning from them to win in life with whatever you choose to dream to do.

6. So You Think You Was Going To Get Away With **THAT** (John 8:32)

   A book exposing the propaganda, spins, lies, and the other secret agendas to control the masses. This book is dedicated to all who were lost in my life as well as those that are still here that are gathering misinformation and confusion that's being used to keep the masses in the dark and not receiving the truth.

7. The Country of the Blind- the One Eyed Man is King: hybrid-man made foods vs natural God made foods (Matt. 15:14) The half truths about foods and the lies and fabrications that are told to us, the masses, to think we are getting proper nutrition.

THE GOLDEN TICKET

Growing up as a child I love watching Willie Wonker and the Chocolate Factory. If you don't remember the movie, Willie Wonker had a chocolate factory that was in the town where he produced massive amounts of chocolate and candy.

Townsmen wondered what went on behind the gates of Mr. Wonka candy production for they never saw him leave the candy factory ever.

One day, Mr. Wonka had an idea to allow a special group of children in for an one day exclusive tour of his candy factory to see how things operated and how Mr. Wonka lived. However, there was a small catch to who would be picked to come inside to take a tour of Willie Wonker's chocolate factory. The catch was that Mr. Wonker would put a golden ticket inside of the wrapper of his famous chocolate bar. Those who got the golden ticket would be admitted to the exclusive once in a life time tour of his factory. No press was allowed inside or recording devices permitted with the child who won an invitation to tour the facility. They could only have one chaperone to accompany them on the tour of Willie's chocolate factory.

The movie was a hit because a poor boy, Charlie, and his old grandfather, Grandpa Joe, in the end inherited Willie's factory because Mr. Wonker wanted to retire and explored the world. The contest was Willie's way of interviewing a potential candidate who would be his predecessor. Mr. Wonker wanted to know if that individual shared the same values as he did before leaving the factory for good.

Well, I explained all of that to say that I too have received my GOLDEN TICKET.

With all that I've been through- the 7 car accidents, being shot at, having guns pulled out on me, mother becoming terminally ill and dying, failed suicide attempt, losing everything and becoming homeless for nine months, and being diagnosed with an incurable disease and beating it, I can honestly say I have the GOLDEN TICKET.

My golden ticket to me is the blood sacrifice that Jesus did at the cross. He died so I could have life here on earth and in eternity. His death gave me the right to be adopted into a family that is rich beyond your or my imagination.

Yes some of the trials I've been through have been scary and dark, cold and frightening, confusing and frustrating but like He promised me "I'll never leave you nor forsake you".

My GOLDEN TICKET was bought at a price that trumps any monetary value so when I am faced with trials that seem tough to bear, I just pull out my GOLDEN TICKET i.e. God's word to remind me that I have all that I need to get through said troubles and this too shall pass whatever I'm going through.

Luke 1:37 says NOTHING is impossible with God. Nothing is an absolute word. With that being said I'm good because like Allstate insurance slogan goes "I'm in good hands".

Trials will come, and trials will go but the constant variable that stays the same is God. He will always be there to take care of me no matter what the situation may be.

If He brought me this far, surely He's not going to leave me in the desert to waste away. We've been through too much to let me go. I just have to hold on and remember the other times and how He showed up and showed out.

Like Charlie, I've inherited the the chocolate factory with streets paved of gold. God says in His Word that I will receive double for my trouble. If the devil has given me one trouble, then for that one trouble I can expect to receive a double-portion blessing!

This was the case with Job. Satan was behind Job's troubles, but when Job responded in faith, God took it upon Himself to restore to Job all that he had lost. The Bible tells us that Job received double in terms of quantity — from 7,000 sheep to 14,000 sheep, 3,000 camels to 6,000 camels, 500 yoke of oxen to 1,000 yoke of oxen and 500 female donkeys to 1,000 female donkeys. And for the children he had lost, God restored in terms of quality — his daughters were the fairest in all the land. (Job 1:2–3, 13–19; 42:12–15)

If Job, who was not under the new covenant, could be blessed with double for his troubles, how much more am I, who's under the new covenant?! In fact, God will not only restore double but triple, fivefold or even sevenfold!

Yes the GREAT I AM is my GOLDEN TICKET that I have forever and ever.

The song sung by Charlie, the young boy in the movie, was spot on accurate, "yes, I got the GOLDEN TICKET!"

Oh Yes It's Personal!

I feel I had to be overweight at one time in my life so that when after losing the weight and keeping it off, I could be a spokesperson, passionate about helping others achieve the same results. I feel the same way with me being diagnosed with multiple sclerosis. I now feel I had to have it because I know am just as passionate with helping those with MS but also other autoimmune diseases that people maybe are going through. The bondage not just physically but mentally, emotionally, psychologically, and most importantly spiritually to give them information and hope to take back their lives.

We are in this together. ALL OF US EVERY SINGLE ONE.

What a Feeling
lyrics from Irene Cara song Flashdance... What A Feeling
READ THE LYRICS SLOWLY AND CLEARLY. Let the lyrics resonate in your mind as you read them.
First when there's nothing
but a slow glowing dream
that your fear seems to hide
deep inside your mind.
All alone I have cried
silent tears full of pride
in a world made of steel,
made of stone.

I was listening to this song one night, not the melody but listening to the lyrics and it inspired me to thinking about the trials I've been through. All of them. The message is very powerful in what it is saying.

Being is believing because with anything it has to become you. I want and wanted to become a health and fitness expert. One of the leading health and fitness professionals in the industry and country.

I am health and fitness no doubt, but I wanted to be the Muhammad Ali, the Michael Jordan, the Babe Ruth, the Vince Lombardi, the Richard Petty and Dale Earnhardt of fitness and health. I wanted to BE health and fitness like those individuals were sport.

Growing up watching the Rocky series training like him afterwards in my room making tons of noise, training for little league/high school/ and college football it brought me joy and tons of peace. Three years ago, I can remember saying repeatedly while training my clients and myself "I will be the face of health and fitness in the entire country", and look at me now. I have mapped out with detail every step I want and wanted to take. I'm making strides towards it despite of the trials I've had to face. Like Princess Asthma said "it's part of the process"!

I believe that God doesn't work off of coincidence, chance, or luck. Everything is played out to its purpose.

In the song it says "I can have it ALL", and I believe that with the help of God I can have it ALL. An abundance not just things and materials but everything-that wife, those kids, that dream position or job, that vacation, that _____ fill in the blank.

You can have it if you believe it.

Walt Disney said "if you can dream it, you can do it".

The famous salesman and motivational speaker, Zig Ziglar said "If you can dream it, then you can achieve it. You will get all you want in life if you help enough other people get what they want.", and I believe that statement to be so true.

Finally, Napoleon Hill said "Whatever the mind can conceive and believe, it can achieve."

I believed that I could get out of the ghetto and experience a life and lifestyle that I watched in movies and television shows like ***Lifestyle of the Rich and Famous***.

I believed that I could excel at sports regardless of even if I didn't start at the same time as everyone else no matter how many hours I had to put in I believed I would catch up and surpass those who where I wanted to be in the end.

I believed my healing would come no matter what the "white coats" were saying or showing on their screens. I just wasn't buying THEIR brand.

I believed that I could transform my physique into one that I thought was pleasing to me which in turn would ooze pleasure to others that saw it and me and maybe wanted the same for themselves, but it started with me and my mind.

What I have learned over these 37 years is nothing is unattainable. The only thing that stands in the way or prevents us from reaching that goal whatever it maybe is patience and our ability to define what mistakes really are. Mistakes are fatal or final. They are just teachers, professors in the classroom of LIFE. We have to identify, embrace, and strategize on the next move. Planning is essential, and without it, you're done. Visualize what you want and how it will be when you obtain it, AND DO NOT STOP UNTIL YOU GET THERE PERIOD.

Just like the song said you have to picture it. Picture having it all no matter if you stumble, it's fall, or fail.

You live like a Viking. The Vikings had a mentality that when they went to take over and conquer a land, they would land and BURN their boat.

What that symbolized mentally and physically was that they were going to conquer this or they were going to die in the process, BUT they **WERE** **NOT** not going back.

Failure is not an option, you have to succeed or else. *__There's no Plan B.__*

So I say whatever the challenge is that you are facing it **MUST** move out the way OR get in agreement with the program that you have outlined.

Viking living. Burn the boat and march forward if that's the thing you want no matter how scary it may be.

Being is believing!

FAME, I'M GONNA LIVE FOREVER

I was a sophomore in high school in English when we were studying and reading the epic novel, ***Beowulf.*** Beowulf is a legendary Geatish hero and later turned king in the epic poem named after him, one of the oldest surviving pieces of literature in the English language.

At end the end Beowulf dies but a statue is made in memory of the fallen warrior and great king.

My English teacher explained that Beowulf would live forever. He was immortal based off the statue.

I didn't understand so I asked if she could elaborate. She did. She explained that Beowulf was immortal because every time a seamen came to shore, he's legend would be told and remembered which made him immortal.

I exclaimed and shouted "I WANT TO BE IMMORTAL"!

Everybody busted in laughter but I was serious. I wanted to find a way where I could become immortal. That thought has been in my head for over twenty years.

Immortality.

Now I have the opportunity to sit with the greats like Beowulf, Achilles, Mae, and many others, but the greatest of them all that really matters and counts is Jesus.

I feel that my trials and test can assist and give someone out there that's reading this hope and a ray of light to get through whatever it is that they may be experiencing. As I've said it before, I feel that I had to be fat as well as I had to have multiple sclerosis so that I can can be effective in providing the best knowledge, data, and information that's available for their needs.

My objective with writing this book was to give those reading this encouragement that we can make it no matter how bad it looks. I hope the objective was met and you laughed at my pain, but more importantly you grab something during our trip together. If crying and clawing to the finish line was how I made it, and it helped someone to still fight and have hope. Then my trials were well worth it every single minute of it.

Mae and Yvette would be well pleased that the hard work that was poured in me has the opportunity to make a difference in this world. They were servant leaders putting others rather it was their kids or just a stranger first.

I got it grandma. I see what you were trying to show momma.

This is my ultimate gift of appreciation to you. Once I learned what immortality was in English class my sophomore year in 1994, twenty one years ago, I promised myself to make them immortal. People would and will know who those precious women were and how they shaped and influenced me.

During the time I was going through the test, I didn't know that my pain, my trials, the things that I had or was about to experience in my life could potentially give hope, strength, encouragement, and laughter to others during their problems and struggles.

It's been an interesting ride, but I wouldn't change a thing.

Now I wouldn't want to retake any of tests, but I wouldn't change not one single answer on the test. It has shaped me into who I am today.

Thank you for walking with me from the ghetto to glory. I'll see you at the finish line.

God bless you all!

Peace and blessings.

Printed in the United States
By Bookmasters